D0311026

touch on issues that cover a wide range of opinions and viewpoints, I want to make it clear that I have no intention to simply promote my views only.

I was surprised that the 30/50 Club was such an exclusive and prestigious group. I might have contributed nothing to Korea's economic growth, but it greatly boosted my pride in my homeland and so I immediately replied to his e-mail.

First, I congratulated him for his 80th birthday, and then I promised that I would send him the written reminiscence that he had requested. I also asked him if he could spend a couple of days with me at my writing studio in Muchangpo Beach in Korea sometime during his visit. I enticed him by promising that I would serve him the spicy fish stew and hand-pulled noodles with clams that Muchangpo was famous for, in addition to my home-made raspberry wine that had aged to perfection.

I wrote this book based on my memories of the conversations I had with him while he stayed with me in Muchangpo for two days and one night. Part I and Part II are the outcome of our conversations.

While reading this book, readers might add their own perspectives to the contents of our conversations or modify them if they desire. Since our conversations

In his e-mail, he explained to me that upon his family's insistence a small gathering was planned in Korea for his 80th birthday to which I was invited. He also asked me to write a short reminiscence of our college days in America which would be included in a booklet to celebrate his birthday. He was asking me, he added, because I was the only writer friend he had.

At the end of the e-mail he congratulated me on Korea joining the "30/50 Club" as the 7th member as of the end of 2018. He added that, while all other member countries of the club were able to build their wealth from exploiting their colonies, (in case of the U.S., a residence colonialism) Korea was able to accumulate wealth even though Korea as a former colony had been harshly exploited.

I googled the 30/50 Club and found out that it refers to countries with over 50 million in population whose per capita income was over thirty thousand dollars. As of today, the members of the club included the United States, Japan, Germany, England, France and Italy, and Korea was the last to join the club.

PROLOGUE

A while ago, I received an e-mail from Professor Kim, whom I hadn't heard from for a long time. Professor Kim and I went to college together in the United States in the late 1960s. He had received his Ph.D. degree in economics and had a rather successful teaching career in America until his retirement. He is now enjoying his retirement in the south of the United States, occasionally contributing columns on international economic affairs to local papers. Since he is a year senior to me, he was approaching his eightieth birthday, which was the reason he sent an e-mail to me.

Part I

KOREA'S NATIONAL LEADERSHIP OUTSHINES THE UNITED STATES' : 1961-2016

Part III

Trade War Between the United States and China: What is Korea's Choice in the War?

Part IV

Economic War Between the US and China, and the Path to Denuclearization of the Korean Peninsula

Part I
Korea's National Leadership Outshines the United States': 1961-2016

Part II
Korea Branching Out to the World, Where is America Headed in the Trump Era?: 2017-2018

30/50 Club

A Dialogue on S. Korea, U.S., China, and N. Korea

(For Truth, Empathy, and Future Harmony!)

by Sang Hwa Hong

Korean Literature Inc.

30/50 Club

A Dialogue on S. Korea, U.S., China, and N. Korea

(For Truth, Empathy, and Future Harmony!)

PATH TO DEBT, PATH TO PROSPERITY

Hong When we compare Korea and the United States, there have been remarkable changes during the past half century.

Kim It's amazing when you think about it, because Korea grew from one of the most impoverished countries into an advanced country and became the 7th member of the 30/50 Club while the United States, which used to be the country with the greatest wealth in history and a national debt of $3 trillion only as late as in early 1980s, became the country with the highest debt ($21 trillion) in 2018.

Hong Can I be straightforward and ask you what happened in the United States during the past half century?

Kim I will answer to the extent of my knowledge. In return, you might want to tell me what had happened in Korea during that time.

Hong I will. In other words, you will tell me what went wrong in the United States and I will tell you what went right in Korea.

Kim Exactly. Now, shall we start? First, you mentioned the last half a century, but how about defining it as the 55 years between 1961 and 2016 for convenience. The reason being, this was the period where the leaders of the two countries showed the most remarkable difference.

Hong The period between 1961 and 2016 means a period between the Kennedy and the Obama administrations in case of the US and the Park Chung-hee and the Park Geun-hye administrations in case of Korea.

Kim That's right. However, before we talk about Kennedy, there is something we must talk about with regard to his predecessor, Eisenhower. On January 17, 1961, Eisenhower gave his farewell address to the American public. Do you remember the content of his televised speech?

Hong I vaguely remember that he used the term 'the military-industrial complex' for the first time.

Kim That's right. He used that word and spent almost the entire farewell address warning about the potential danger of the military-industrial complex on American society. That showed the intensity of the sense of crisis Eisenhower felt about it.

Hong Did Eisenhower turn out to be right?

Kim I would say he was absolutely right. If you look at the records of the United States' involvement in wars that followed, the United States sent troops to wars in Vietnam, Afghanistan and Iraq, and these are only the major wars. Looking back, all these wars didn't do anything good in terms of the national interest. Instead, they have been the main cause of astronomical national debts and the moral decline of America, not to mention the tragic sacrifices of American youths and local people .

Hong How massive is the scale of the US military-industrial complex?

Kim If I may briefly explain, the GDP of the United States accounts for a quarter of the GDP of the entire world, and the United States government is spending at least 5 percent of the GDP on the US military. This amount is close to half of all military expenses of the world. (For your reference, Korea spends about 2.5 percent of its GDP on the military.) Such a mammoth military-industrial complex is constantly on the lookout for places where war is likely to happen in the world and starts war one way or another.

Hong I guess Korea is one of the potential battlefields.

Kim No question about it. In that sense, there is a great significance in the statement made by Korean foreign minister in 2018 when she said, "There cannot be another war on the Korean Peninsula."

Hong What is the significance?

Kim It means she declared "Don't even think about

starting a war in Korea." In other words, she declared to countries around the world that Korea now became an autonomous, advanced country.

Hong I guess she meant to declare it to the military-industrial complex of the United States.

Kim You are right. On top of that, she also meant to warn certain power circles inside Japan, China and Russia that were secretly hoping the United States would bomb North Korea.

Hong Why was that?

Kim Take Japan for example. The Japanese brand Sony started to decline because of the Korean brand Samsung. That means, Korea is an unnerving competitor to Japan in many ways. And also there are groups of people in China and Russia who tend to favor the US's bombing of North Korea, believing that it will deprive the US of its opportunity to contain China and Russia.

Hong I see. It's a truly terrifying world. With that background in mind, let's talk about the leadership of the leaders of Korea and the United States between 1961 and 2016. First off, please tell me about the leaders who ruled the United States for the 18 years between 1961 and 1979.

Kim Is there any special reason you specify that period?

Hong Because it is the period marked by the long 18-year seizure of power by Park Chung-hee from 1961 when he staged a military coup on May 16, to 1979 when he was assassinated by the director of the KCIA (Korean Central Intelligence Agency).

Kim I see. Then, let me talk about the leadership of the United States during the administrations of Kennedy, Johnson, Nixon, and Carter (1961-1981). Of these four presidents, I will give my specific accounts of Kennedy and Nixon, because in my opinion, they left a significant influence on the United States.

KENNEDY'S TRADE EXPANSION ACT, PARK CHUNG-HEE'S HEAVY CHEMICAL INDUSTRY

Kim Kennedy was sworn in on January 20, 1961 and under him, Congress passed the Trade Expansion Act in 1962 and opened the US markets to Japan and Germany too quickly and too generously. Consequently, the two countries of Japan and Germany—whose massive industrial potentials were on a par with the United States (as proven by World War II)—were able to make forays into the United States and deal a devastating blow to the US manufacturing industries with significant impact on the US heavy industry in particular.

Hong Did Kennedy's opening of the US market signify

a reduction in tariffs?

Kim Mainly so. GATT (General Agreement on Tariffs and Trade) was formed in 1948 as an intergovernmental organization whose overall purpose was to reduce or eliminate trade barriers such as tariffs and quotas that could pose an obstacle to trading goods among countries. Before GATT was signed, an average tariff was about 70 percent, which means the price of a foreign import was about twice the actual import cost on the domestic market. After GATT was signed, the US tariffs started to go down, and the reduction rate started to accelerate as a result of the Kennedy administration's policy on the reduction of tariffs. This trend continued even after his death until it dropped to slightly over 10 percent.

Hong What could have motivated Kennedy to reduce tariffs?

Kim It was Kennedy's naive idealism, combined with the challenges from Communist countries (the Soviet Union's launching of Sputnik, the first artificial satellite, in 1957 and the Cuban Revolution led by Fidel Castro in 1960).

Hong It is hard to fully grasp the assertion that the heavy industries of Germany and Japan dealt a devastating blow to the heavy industry of the United States all because of the reduction of tariffs alone.

Kim If competing on equal ground without the high tariffs of the United States, the heavy industries of Japan and Germany had enough prowess to compete successfully with those of the United States.

Hong What were the reasons?

Kim First off, those two countries had lower wages because their per capita incomes were comparatively lower than that of the United States. Secondly, they were able to secure newly developed producer goods marked by high productivity, and third, there was a difference in the consciousness of workers.

Hong What do you mean by the difference in the consciousness of workers?

Kim Take the consciousness of Japanese workers for example. Even though Japan was the victim of two atomic bombs, war was not over as far as they were concerned. They knew they were winning the post-war war if the television sets they made were installed in the living rooms of American households and if the automobiles they made were preferred by American consumers. The same attitudes applied to German workers, even though the intensity might have been lower than that of the Japanese workers.

Hong I have a question lingering in my mind. Could the United States drop an atomic bomb on Germany as well?

Kim That's the question to be answered by the American conscience. My guess is, it would not be an easy answer. It is true that the Japanese workers might have harbored the same question in their hearts, and that it helped the recovery of the post-war Japanese economy.

Hong Would it be possible that the United States was being more generous to Japan because that imaginary question was poking at the American conscience?

Kim Let's drop the subject, because racial discrimination is an issue that is interlocked with nasty human nature.

Hong Fair enough. Then, I guess it is safe to say that some of the US heavy industries were occupied by two enemy countries the US had defeated in the war. How about accepting it as the generosity of the United States that supports the post-war recovery of the defeated countries?

Kim American citizens became the victims of damages that went beyond a simple generosity without even realizing it.

Hong What damages?

Kim In the hearts of ordinary Americans, the images of the German-made Mercedes and the Japanese-made Toyota were engraved deeply as automobiles with outstanding performance and automobiles they could purchase with confidence respectively.

Hong There is nothing wrong about teaching

Americans that they had lessons to learn, is there?

Kim There is nothing wrong. However, it made them forget about the history that could be forgiven but should never be forgotten by humanity.

Hong Can you elaborate?

Kim What I mean is that historic facts such as the genocide committed at the Auschwitz concentration camp and the massacre committed in Nanjing are overshadowed by the logos of Mercedes and Toyota, and the American citizens gradually became oblivious to these catastrophies.

Hong What substantial changes did happen with regard to the US trade situation?

Kim The expansion of tariff reduction negotiations that started before the death of Kennedy culminated in the Kennedy Round which was signed in 1967. Less than ten years later in 1976, the United States recorded a trade deficit for the first time. On the other hand, Japan registered surpluses in their trade balance for the first time in 1965, and in 1988, Japan's trade surplus recorded $48 billion.

Hong I guess that made it difficult to tell the winners from the losers of World War II.

Kim It might as well be the outcome resulting from Kennedy's naïve romantic idealism and his lack of experience as a leader

●●●

Kim Could you set aside what happened in America now and tell me about what happened in Korea at the time?

Hong A few months after the inauguration of Kennedy in 1961, the then-military general Park Chung-hee led a military coup on May 16. Park graduated from a teachers' college and worked as a teacher in a girl's middle school before he entered the Manchukuo Imperial Army and completed its two-year course. After graduating top of his class, he was granted the privilege of transferring to the Imperial Japanese Army Academy in Japan. Upon graduation in 1944, he became a Japanese officer and served in the Japanese Manchukuo Imperial Army until Korea became liberated on August 15, 1945.

Kim It is amazing how a man with that kind of background could have decided to push forward with the heavy and chemical industries drive when Korea was in such a destitute state at the time. Was it just the naive passion of a soldier?

Hong When Park Chung-hee was transferred to the Imperial Japanese Army Academy, all the newly admitted students including Park were given a chance to tour the heavy and chemical industrial facilities in Japan. It is said that it was during this tour that Park Chung-hee, a farmer's son in his early 20s at the time, came to believe firmly that only the heavy and chemical industries drive was going to be the engine for the reconstruction of the country.

Kim I doubt international aid organizations would have willingly agreed to heavily invest in the heavy and chemical industries of Korea at the time. Without help from aid organizations, as it had been impossible for Korea to accumulate capital, Korea would not have been able to pull it off on its own.

Hong A winner of the Nobel Prize of 2001 in Economics once said that when the World Bank suggested agriculture and light industry as development basis, Korea answered "No, thank you," and decisively rejected it. At any rate, about a decade after the military coup, or around the time when the Vietnam War was coming to an end, Korea became a country with its own steel foundry, oil refinery plant, ship-building plant and numerous highways.

Kim The Vietnam War started during the Kennedy administration and ended in the Nixon administration. So, shall we return to the Nixon era that started in 1974?

Hong All right. For we know, the Park Chung-hee era lasted throughout the Nixon era and came to an end in 1979 during the Carter era when Park was assassinated by his subordinate who was the chief of the Korean Central Intelligence Agency at the time.

Kim I wonder what went through his mind when he was killed after having devoted himself solely to the modernization of his fatherland while taking criticism for oppressing human rights.

Hong I serialized a short story titled *President Park's Last Words* in commemoration of the 20th anniversary of his death in 1999 on a daily newspaper in four parts. Written in the form of a monologue, I imagined what must have gone through his mind from the moment he was shot till the moment he took his last breath.

Kim Can you send me a copy of the story?

Hong Sure, I can. (Attached as Appendix 1)

MILITARY-INDUSTRIAL COMPLEX OF THE KENNEDY ERA STARTS A WAR

Hong Among the incidents that happened in America during the 18-year period from 1961 to 1979, one could say that the Vietnam War was the event that had the greatest impact on American society, wouldn't you say?

Kim I would say so. The Vietnam War blew up into a major issue in 1963 during the Kennedy administration and it lasted throughout the Johnson administration. The conflict lasted for a whopping ten years if we consider the Paris Peace Accord signed in 1973 as its conclusion, even though the Fall of Saigon happened two years later.

Hong I reckon it cost America significantly, didn't it?

Kim In 1963, 16,000 US troops were deployed in Vietnam, but the number shot up to 100,000 in just a few years. By the time the war came to an end, the United States sustained more than 58,000 casualties. In terms of the cost of the war, the US spent multi-trillion dollars.

Hong How did Kennedy justify the US involvement in the war?

Kim He used the Domino theory, which was about the inevitability of the communization of Vietnam creating a domino effect and communizing all of East Asia.

Hong Did the theory turn out to be correct?

Kim As Eisenhower pointed out in his farewell address, we have to assume that the invisible power of the military-industrial complex was at work.

Hong What choices could volatile neighbor countries make to avoid a possible military clash?

Kim The only solution for the involved parties

is negotiation. If involved parties insist on confrontation and remain hostile to each other, they are likely to become the prey of military-industrial complex (MIC) and a war is unavoidable. The consequence is the instantaneous destruction of social overhead capital facilities that take decades, even centuries to build up, not to mention the loss of countless lives. Take a look at the Middle Eastern countries for example. They are reduced to ashes after fighting with their neighbors or fighting each other within their own countries.

Hong The current Korean government knew what they needed to do when they declared "no war on the Korean peninsula."

Kim I would say Korea threw a hard punch at the MIC for the first time since Eisenhower warned of the danger of MIC in his farewell address of 1961.

Hong I've never realized what a dangerous threat the MIC really is.

Kim There is something Eisenhower's daughter said in an interview after the death of her father. She said her father often lamented that, considering how the MIC was trying to control him (Eisenhower), a man with a military background, he was extremely worried how the presidents without a military background would be manipulated by the MIC.

Hong Kennedy, Clinton, George W. Bush (the son), and Obama are the US Presidents without a real military background. Is that the reason wars broke out while they were in office? Because they did not understand the tragedy of war.

Kim It might have been a factor.

Hong Trump has never been in the army as well. Therefore, he is likely to have little understanding of the terror of war and therefore more likely to start a war.

Kim That's the reason we have to give a bigger hand to the female Korean foreign minister in Moon Jae-in's administration who was the first to declare "no war on the Korean Peninsula".

Hong When you think about it, two Korean women could take the credit for having made Korea a dignified, advanced country.

Kim I know one woman who made Korea a country not to be taken lightly to countries that never treated Korea seriously, but I wonder who the other woman is and what she has accomplished.

Hong The other woman is the one who helped enact a bill, so-called 'Kim Young Ran Act' capping one-hour lecture fee to $500 for example, that virtually transformed Korea with reputation of corruption to one of the cleanest countries in the world.

Kim I believe there are numerous people who accuse you of being a feminist.

Hong If I am, it is because Korean women's DNA is far superior to that of Korean males.

Kim Why is that so superior?

Hong It has something to do with Korea's long history of oppression and perseverance. It is the same reason Jews are superior to other people, because the Jewish also have a history marked by oppression and perseverance.

Kim I guess soon Korea will move beyond a male

and female equality society to a female-superior society.

Hong It will come naturally, sooner or later. It is already happening in the sports world, and soon the trend will spread throughout society beginning with legal circles. When it happens, Korea will become one of the world leaders, wouldn't you agree?

THE ERA OF NIXON AND PARK CHUNG-HEE, THE LOSSES AND GAINS OF THE VIETNAM WAR

Kim Our conversation got sidetracked a little bit. We were talking about the Vietnam War, and the reason we talked about war was to point out what the US Presidents have done wrong.

Hong The Vietnam War dealt a serious blow to the US in terms of casualties as well as the economy and morality. But for Korea, the war gave a big boost to the economy even though it was at the cost of sacrificing precious lives.

Kim Formally speaking, the Vietnam War was a war engaged in by multi-national forces. But there were only two countries that actually took part in it: the United States and Korea, which sent a military force of 50,000 troops. What did Korea gain from the war?

Hong Korea made a significant economic gain because the Korean sappers, who were deployed to Vietnam and experienced the construction of roads in Vietnam laid the groundwork for Korean construction companies to make forays into the Middle Eastern markets. And the financing of construction for the Gyeongbu Expressway also might have had something to do with Korea's involvement in the Vietnam War.

Kim Then something truly amazing happened. I've heard that one of the leading corporations in Vietnam as of 2017 is Samsung Electronics' subsidiary in Vietnam. Samsung's Vietnamese operation is hiring over 100,000 locals and, according to what I hear, their export of smartphones accounts for 25 percent of all exports from Vietnam.

Hong Korean *chaebol* corporations are often the target of criticism in Korea, but in truth, there are many things that would not have been possible if not for the sweat and blood of management and employees of those *chaebol* corporations. I think people should have the decency to appreciate and applaud their hard work sometimes.

Kim I'm sure it wouldn't have been possible had there been no trust between the two countries, and that makes me wonder: How were they able to build trust with each other? Particularly considering how Korea's involvement in the Vietnam War must have left many Vietnamese holding a grudge against Koreans?

Hong Well, I think it's because both countries have a positive common ground. Both Korea and Vietnam share the same Confucianism-based sets of values, such as honoring elders, respecting honor, and worshipping ancestors. Korea is the only country in the world where Confucianism remains alive in its original form. Korea accepted Buddhism and Christianity with its foundation built upon Confucianism.

Kim As far as I know, Ho Chi Minh was a

Confucianism scholar and so was his father. It seems to me that the respect of the intellectuals from around the world for Ho Chi Minh as the Father of Vietnam has a lot to do with his background.

Hong Confucian ideology set aside, there is a reason Koreans truly respect the Vietnamese. It is that Vietnam defeated on its soil seemingly invincible armies of the United States and China in the 1960s and late 1970s. From the perspective of Koreans, the United States helped Korea to avoid turning into a communist country in the 1950s, and in the case of China, Korea has been under its dominance throughout history because Korea has been either in a brotherhood relationship with China or a relationship between the ruler and the ruled.

Kim Then, how did Vietnam come to respect Korea?

Hong The first reason must be Korea's impressive economic growth. The second might have been the Hallyu (Korean-wave) dramas. And more than anything, their respect must be the manifestation of their appreciation for Koreans who acknowledge the Vietnamese as a strong people who fought against the United States, the world's strongest super power, and won.

●●●

Kim Nixon should be held accountable for the communization of Vietnam, even though he took credit for having ended the Vietnam War. But to tell from the perspective of the United States, it is not easy to identify damages the United States suffered as the result of the communization of Vietnam. However, one cannot deny that Nixon caused significant damages to the United States when he ended the military draft (1973).

Hong What damages did he cause?

Kim I can identify three damages. First, the young generation of America lost the opportunity to discipline themselves mentally and physically. The second, the military could be mobilized not for a dire national security reason but for a less serious reason such as the nation's economic interest. And the third damage is that the declined exposure to patriotism fostered their younger generation's greed for the get-rich-quick mentality.

Hong I can relate to the first reason you identified. Young Koreans who went through the grueling military training and discipline either as officers or privates were able to compete with young Japanese and Americans who hadn't had the same military experience and triumphed over them. These young Koreans are the ones who built Samsung of Vietnam, skyscrapers in Malaysia and Vietnam, and highways that run across the deserts in the Middle East. Their power must have come from it, don't you think?

Kim You are correct. On top of that, the fierce sense of competition that Koreans experienced in their high school days while applying to the notoriously competitive Korean college admission system might have been another big contributor. For we know that high school days, along with pre-school days, are a very important time for brain development. Compared to workers from other countries, Korean workers are definitely capable of being more productive.

Hong I can also understand the second damage you mentioned. The United States participated in a number of wars after 1973, not crucial to the U.S. security and I assume it has something to do with the ending of the military draft. But I wonder what motivated Nixon to end the draft?

Kim The ending of the draft was a campaign promise Nixon made as he ran for reelection in 1972 to win the young American voters. After he was reelected, the promise was realized after many ups and downs. His move was met by strong objections, because people were concerned that the end of the draft would mean the United States military turning into a mercenary group.

Hong When you think about it, the leaders of Korea in the early 1970s were more shocked by the possibility of the US draft policy coming to an end than the possibility of Vietnam turning into a communist regime. It was because they feared that, had there been another war on the Korean peninsula, a US force that consisted of mercenaries would not be as committed to fighting for us as they did during the Korean War.

Kim Is that the cause behind the birth of Park Chung-hee's Yushin regime?

Hong That, and the wide-spread expectation of Korean left-wing intellectuals in academic circles that Korea would be the next to become communized following Vietnam.

Kim But wouldn't you say the Yushin regime was too oppressive?

Hong You can say that. But after Vietnam's fall to communism, the left-leaning Korean political faction called NL (National Liberation Front) was showing signs that they believed the world was already theirs. Anyhow, the Yushin regime came to an end because of a gunshot fired by the head of the Korean Central intelligence agency in 1979.

Kim Then, what is the legacy of Park Chung-hee's Yushin regime other than the extreme oppression of human rights?

Hong I can identify two very important legacies. One is that during the 7-year Yushin administration (1972-1979), Korean economy reached the "take-off" stage by recording over 11 percent annual economic growth. The second is that the gap between the South and the North's economic power grew so big that the pro-North forces in the South lost their influence in South Korea.

Kim I see. Is there any academic paper about the accomplishments of Park Chung-hee? I want to delve more deeply into them.

Hong I included some newspaper articles in my short story I mentioned. It was a collection of articles regarding Park Chung-hee's accomplishments divided into different categories. I will send it to you later. (Attached as Appendix 2)

Kim I appreciate it. I will read them carefully. And

lastly, I want to ask you. What do you think about the third damage caused by the ending of draft that I mentioned previously?

Hong You were right on when you mentioned the young people's declining interest in patriotism and their worship of money. I cannot think of any better method to raise young people's awareness to their patriotism than the military experience. Without a strong sense of one's fatherland, young people naturally become overwhelmed by mercantilism of capitalism and driven into the worship of money.

Kim Perhaps that's the reason young American brains are flocking to Wall Street and dreaming of getting rich quickly, without stopping at any activities that are close to being frauds....

Hong The ending of the draft deprived young Americans of an opportunity to discipline themselves both physically and mentally. What truly matters for them is to have big dreams that have nothing to do with monetary motivation and living with those big dreams. But they were deprived of the opportunity to do it.

CARTER PREVENTS THE POSSIBILITY OF A WAR ON THE KOREAN PENINSULA

Kim Now, let's skip to the Reagan administration (1981-1989). Reagan is known to have practiced so-called finance capitalism, and in fact, we can say that it's continued for 36 years until early 2017 when Trump took power.

Hong What are the characteristics of that long period?

Kim One of the characteristics is the fact that those from Wall Street constituted the core power group in the United States.

Hong Isn't there anything particular to note about the single term of the Carter administration (1977-1981) that preceded the Reagan administration?

Kim If I may point out something, I would say it has to do with the role Carter had played as the former US President during the Clinton administration. Carter had a meeting with Kim Il-sung in 1994 and struck a deal with Kim which effectively stopped the US government from launching an attack on the North's nuclear reactor at Yongbyon. In that sense, he is someone Koreans should appreciate.

Hong Since you mentioned it, let me ask you a question. What would have happened if the US government went on to bomb Yongbyon at the time?

Kim The Korean peninsula would have been permanently leveled beyond recovery. That's what was disclosed in many interviews by the then US ambassador to Korea, James Laney, the commander-in-chief US forces Korea, General Gary Luck, and the special envoy for the U.S. Department of State, Robert Gallucci.

Hong The complete destruction of the Korean peninsula is a scenario that could have happened if we assume that the North responded with military action to the bombing, isn't it?

Kim At the time, North Korea had about 500 artillery pieces dug deep into the mountains on the border. If those artillery pieces were used to launch an attack at Seoul, it could have resulted in the casualties of millions of Seoul citizens, and according to analysis by experts, more casualties were likely to result from radioactive fallout than from the bombing per se.

Hong When you said radioactive, do you mean the radioactive fallout that would have resulted if the US bombed the nuclear reactor in Yongbyon, North Korea?

Kim Exactly. In South Korea, there are over 10 nuclear power plants.

Hong Would the Clinton administration have considered that risk when it decided to launch an attack against the nuclear reactor at Yongbyon?

Kim They made the decision based on two incorrect assumptions. First, they assumed that North Korea would not respond with military action even if the US bombed Yongbyon.

Hong On what basis did they make that assumption?

Kim According to the special envoy Robert Gallucci, the United States was supposed to deliver a clear message to the North Korean regime before attacking Yongbyon and the supposed message was "the bombing was not targeting the regime change," which in essence meant, "we will protect the current North Korean regime."

Hong You mean they wanted the North to stay put because Kim Il-sung's military response would bring about their own downfall. It was a truly dangerous idea, considering how it would not have been easy for the regime to control commanders on the front line had the North been attacked. What was the second incorrect assumption?

Kim They assumed that they could minimize the radiation leak if they went for a so-called precision attack when they bombed Yongbyon. They thought they could avoid the risk of having a radiation leak from bombing Yongbyon reducing the Korean peninsula to ruins.

Hong Why was that a wrong assumption?

Kim Let me introduce you a conversation that happened between the then-United States Ambassador to South Korea James Laney and the then-commander of U.S. forces in Korea, General Gary Luck, around the time when the US was about to bomb North Korea. Ambassador Laney was the president of Emory University before he was appointed the US Ambassador to Korea, and General Luck was a highly-educated military leader who received a bachelor's degree in engineering and a doctorate in business administration.

Hong I'm curious about their conversation.

Kim When Ambassador Laney asked about the precision attack, General Luck gave him a straightforward, simple answer. He answered that in the history of mankind, there had never been any attack on a nuclear power plant that was in operation, and no matter how precise the attack might be, you simply could not stop radiation leaking once it was bombed. His point was that the Korean peninsula would be instantly exposed.

Hong It reminds me of the Fukushima Daiichi nuclear disaster. It left devastating damages even though it was caused by a simple blackout incident when a tsunami damaged the generator….

Kim That's the reason I'm telling you Carter deserves a statue for what he did.

Hong Was the role Carter played that significant?

Kim According to the special envoy Gallucci, Carter called the White House from Pyongyang at around the time when Clinton was in talks with his security team that included the US Secretary of Defense to make the final decision on launching a strike at the North. According to his account, Gallucci left the conference room to take the call from Carter and was told on the phone about Carter having struck an agreement with Kim Il-sung.

Hong That was a truly perilous moment.

Kim That didn't mean the end of the crisis, because Clinton could have ignored the agreement Carter had made with Kim. At that time, Carter's visit to the North was not approved by the US government. He simply accepted Kim Il-sung's invitation as a private citizen.

Hong But Clinton honored that agreement, fortunately, I assume.

Kim He had to, because immediately following Carter's call to Washington, CNN was breaking the news about the agreement reached between Carter and Kim Il-sung in Pyongyang in the form of a live interview.

Hong So, Clinton could not start a war because he was mindful of possible criticisms coming from the international community. Clinton is a truly heartless leader, because I'm sure he was well aware of the danger the Korean peninsula was exposed to.

Kim He was truly a heartless person. Had there not been intervention by Carter, the Korean people would have been annihilated forever.

Hong During the 2016 presidential campaign race, Trump referred to his rival Hilary Clinton as "Crooked Hilary." What was the basis of that name calling?

Kim Mr. and Mrs. Clinton raked in close to $10 million in paid speeches in just a year leading up to the election. They made about 30 paid speeches, and they received $330,000 on average per speech that was barely an hour long. The money that they received was, in effect, advanced bribes paid to somebody who they believed was going to become the next president.

Hong Compared to that, Korea is a rather clean country because a speech by any former government official is capped at around $500 per hour.

Kim That shows how corrupt the United States is. Corruption concealed under the cloak of legitimacy is prevalent. For example, the number of lobbyists registered on behalf of pharmaceutical companies outnumbers the number of Congress members. That's the reason drugs are so expensive in America.

Hong What about the corruption of Chinese leaders?

Kim It is bad in America, but it is worse among Chinese leaders. It is to the point where almost all

Chinese leaders and their families are reportedly richer than successful Chinese businessmen.

Hong You said that the Korean peninsula avoided Clinton's attack in 1994 thanks to the agreement Carter had reached with Kim, but why did the agreement between Carter and Kim Il-sung end up falling apart later?

Kim Bush included North Korea as the "Axis of Evil" along with Iran and Iraq in his State of the Union address in 2002.

Hong What was the background of it?

Kim The term "military-industrial complex", which Eisenhower had used in his farewell address, comes to my mind. Probably it was because this "monster" had to constantly come up with more countries where it could start a war, but the two countries of Iran and Iraq alone did not bear proportional balance both geologically or numerically. So, Bush ended up with adding North Korea to the list for them. Adding another country also worked better in terms of the flow of his address.

Hong You mean Clinton was being the puppet of plutocrats and Bush was dancing to the MIC's tune.

Kim That would be what it was. America is known to have the best procedure to select the best leaders, but considering those were the leaders America had chosen, you can imagine what leaders of other countries would be like, can't you?

Hong It is terrifying.

Kim No leaders of the world should be trusted. Almost all leaders of the worlds are individuals who couldn't care less about the sacrifices of the people of other countries as long as they work for the interest of their own people and their own political status.

REAGAN'S FINANCE CAPITALISM, CHUN DOO-HWAN'S SUSTAINED ECONOMIC GROWTH

Kim We started talking about the accomplishments of Reagan, and then we suddenly changed subject to the possibility of war on the Korean peninsula and ended up talking about it for longer than expected. But there is an issue we must point out here, because, no matter what, the priority of Korea is keeping war from ever happening on the Korean peninsula.

Hong Any Korean would agree with that. The economy can either go up or down, but if a war breaks out on the Korean peninsula, the Korean people might never recover from the consequences and everybody knows it.

Kim In fact, for nearly 36 years beginning in 1981 when Reagan took office to 2017 when Obama left office and Trump was sworn in, America was under the rule of finance capitalism where virtually entire industries including the manufacturing industry were under the control of financial industry.

Hong That explains the current situation where the foundation of the American manufacturing industries became so flawed that the US could not even make a decent flat screen TV anymore.

Kim That's right. The elite group from the American financial industry was the de facto ruler for those 36 long years that cover the administrations of three Republican presidents and two Democratic presidents.

Hong What do you mean by the elite group that was the de facto ruler of America?

Kim Donald T. Regan had worked for the investment company Merrill Lynch as CEO before he joined the Reagan administration and served Ronald

Reagan as the US Secretary of the Treasury and the White House Chief of Staff from 1981 to 1986. There were seven other government officials who had worked in the financial industry before joining the administrations after Reagan left office and controlled many succeeding U.S. Presidents behind the curtain.

Hong Can you tell me who they were?

Kim They were Alan Greenspan, Robert Rubin, Lawrence Summers and Henry Paulson for the period between 1987 and 2006 (some of them served only a part of this period), and Lawrence Summers, Ben Bernanke and Timothy Geithner for the period between 2007 and 2016 (again, some of them served only a part of this period). They are the ones who created the plutocracy of the United States.

Hong Then, can you tell me about the accomplishments of Reagan, who started the so-called finance capitalism that lasted for 36 years? After that, I will talk about the accomplishments of Chun Doo-hwan whose term ran roughly in parallel to the Reagan era.

Kim All right. But I guess I should talk more about his maladministration cases than his accomplishments. After being sworn into office, President Ronald Reagan fired more than 10,000 air traffic controllers who belonged to the Professional Air-Traffic Controllers Association and successfully incapacitated the air controllers' labor union. Companies jumped on the bandwagon of this sweeping move and started disbanding labor unions until the number of American workers belonging to unions in private sectors dropped from 30 percent to just 10 percent.

Hong Isn't the declining membership of labor unions good for companies?

Kim It isn't necessarily so. Fewer labor unions mean less transparency of corporate management and more plutocratic despotism of business leaders. Therefore, for the first time in US history, companies became prey to hedge funds, and predatory corporate raiders were able to fatten their pockets with the money they made from companies that they broke up and sold off. In addition, some companies were able to grow into mammoths through merger and acquisition (M&A) while numerous people were laid off during the process.

Hong I see Korea is in an advantageous position in that sense for having powerful labor unions, as long as they are not inclined to turn to unreasonable strikes.

Kim That is for sure. If the financial institutions in America had labor unions as powerful as those of Korea, there wouldn't have been such unethical predatory lending or performance-based bonus parties for corporate executives.

Hong I see how the seed for the financial crisis that hit the United States in 2008 was planted by Reagan's finance capitalism.

Kim You can say that. In the end, Americans barely managed to resolve the crisis by resorting to higher national debt, but that means they burdened their following generations. How was

Korea during the years Reagan was in power in America?

●●●

Hong After Park Chung-hee was assassinated towards the end of 1979, Korea went through a short period of turbulence until Chun Doo-hwan, the then-major general who was appointed commander of Security Command under Park Chung-hee, seized power.

Kim I understand there was a serious violation of human rights as he rose to power, is that right?

Hong I know that there were some serious casualties of innocent citizens in Gwangju when army enforcers of martial law brutally suppressed demonstrations that took place in the city. But perhaps for that very reason, Chun Doo-hwan was able to achieve many remarkable things.

Kim A scholar once argued that, when lacking legitimacy, a ruler will try to compensate for it with efficacy. I wonder if that theory can be applied in this case.

Hong At any rate, Chun Doo-hwan left some remarkable accomplishments in the eight years of his presidency before leaving office in 1988, all despite numerous domestic and international crises such as the oil crisis (1981) and the Rangoon bombing (1983).

Kim I'm curious about his accomplishments, because he had such a bad image in the general public.

Hong For a starter, he made rapid economic growth supported by sound finance and price stability. He was able to keep inflation under control by freezing public finance and the budget for the first time since the founding of the Republic, a move that turned out to have strengthened national competitiveness and allowed Korea to maintain the same impressive growth rate of the previous Park Chung-hee administration. Some people claim that this was the starting point of Korea's traditional soundness of national finance.

Kim What are the other accomplishments?

Hong During his presidency, significant progress was made in laying the groundwork for a social safety network. The national pension system and universal health insurance programs are some of the examples.

Kim Korea's current health insurance program is among the best in the world in terms of its efficacy, because anybody can get to see world-class doctors at college-affiliated hospitals for about three minutes for their medical needs at less than $10, as long as they are willing to wait for about two days. Some of my friends in America are coming back to Korea for that reason. It is a program you cannot even imagine in any country around the world.

Hong The successful bidding for the 1988 summer Olympics in Seoul should also be included in his accomplishments, because Korea became the first Asian country to host the Olympics since the 1964 Tokyo Olympics in Japan and it greatly enhanced Korea's prestige in the international community as a result.

THE ERA OF BUSH, THE FATHER: THE COLLAPSE OF THE FORMER SOVIET UNION AVERTS A BIG DISASTER

Kim Reagan was succeeded by George H.W. Bush (1989-1993), who left office after finishing one four-year term and was succeeded by Clinton (1993-2001). The father Bush's biggest achievement should be the collapse of the Soviet Union, the unrivaled leader of the Communist Bloc.

Hong The collapse of the Soviet Union was a shock to most humanities scholars, for the truth was, their common endeavor was to minimize sacrifices that would result from the arrival of communism. The majority of the world population belonging to the working class, they considered the communization of the world was only a matter of time.

Kim What about scholars in the literary area? Did they feel the same?

Hong If you say scholars in the literary area, they are mostly literary critics. If I may summarize the attitude of many of them, it was, "Who cares about lousy stories of love when nuclear war is going to break out at any minute? The duty of critics should be to praise literature that promotes the arrival of communism."

Kim Perhaps that explains the reason that Korean literature has been leaning towards the Left, because there have been many Korean intellectuals who follow the leading trend of ideas of the intellectuals of the world.

Hong This might be a silly question, but what brought down the former Soviet Union?

Kim What do you mean silly? It is a question to which even the most erudite scholars can't provide a clear answer. It is understandable, considering how Communism that people believed would eventually replace Capitalism collapsed almost suddenly after 70 years of existence, starting with Soviet Russia.

Hong Even until the early 1980s, the dominant prediction was that Communism led by the former Soviet Union would triumph over Capitalism led by the United States. This prediction was particularly dominant in the circle of intellectuals of ivory towers.

Kim Back then, Western intellectuals didn't know how corrupt the Soviet leaders really were. It was to the point where people in the Soviet Union didn't believe anything about the Chernobyl disaster that their own news media were reporting. They only believed the announcements made by The International Atomic Energy Agency (IAEA). Even Soviet leaders could not trust each other.

Hong How on earth did it go that far?

Kim When you think about it, a society that doesn't acknowledge private ownership is destined to lose the sense of competition, and without competition, people become lazy and lazy people means declining economy. Declining economy translates into increasing corruption. Nevertheless, the Soviet Union kept competing with the United States in the arms race until their economy was pushed to the edge of a cliff. The Soviet Union couldn't even afford to maintain properly its nuclear power plant.

Hong How bad was the corruption among the Soviet leaders?

Kim It was beyond words. For example, Mikhail Gorbachev's predecessor and the former General Secretary of the Central Committee of the Communist Party of the Soviet Union, Leonid Brezhnev, collected luxury Western cars for a hobby. In a society where freedom of press is not guaranteed, the leaders are destined to become corrupt.

Hong Anyway, it was extremely fortunate that we were able to avoid a nuclear war between the United States and the Soviet Union, which was a big concern among intellectuals.

Kim I would say it brought hope to humanity once again. At the time, the Soviet Union had approximately 5,000 nuclear warheads aiming at the US mainland and was waiting for the order to open fire to come from Kremlin.

Hong Who should take the credit for having averted a disaster against humanity?

Kim I'd say the credit should go to Mikhail Gorbachev who was the leader of the Soviet Union when it collapsed, and his wife Raisa.

Hong Why Raisa?

Kim That's just my hunch. Gorbachev would not have been able to make such a daring decision alone. Ms. Raisa Gorbacheva must have played a critical role in the decision because, being a philosophy and sociology scholar, she was capable of humanitarian thinking, and she also had feminine sensitivity.

Hong In other words, you can say that the power of a single woman named Raisa might have contributed to turning those 5,000 nuclear warheads away from the United States.

Kim But what's the use of reducing the number of nuclear warheads from 5,000 to zero? The US military budget has kept increasing even after the collapse of the Soviet Union, which had been their main enemy, and the US also kept building more aircraft carriers that cost close to $10 billion per piece.

Hong What is the reason for that?

Kim I would say the tyranny of the MIC is to blame. Korea has to remain alert and cautious if we don't want to fall prey to their tyranny. Eisenhower had a good reason to warn about the MIC in his farewell address in 1961. It was a warning that the US democracy could be seized by the MIC.

CLINTON'S PLUTOCRACY BURIES THE US ECONOMY IN CRISIS

Kim The finance capitalism of the Clinton administration (1993-2001) that started in 1993, which was after the end of the confrontational structure between the East and the West, or the fall of the former Soviet Union in 1991, showed signs of change. In the Clinton administration, finance capitalism became more heavily lopsided towards the "finance" part, now that the competitive structure with Communism was gone. It now became closer to plutocracy.

Hong While the finance capitalism was more about finance dominating the manufacturing industry in its nature, plutocracy was about a situation where society is under the dominance of the super-rich, if I understand it right.

Kim It is a simplified definition of it. Anyhow, the plutocracy of the United States that was born under the Clinton administration came to its completion in the Obama administration (2009-2017), because it was in 2010 that the independent political action committee, commonly called "Super PAC", became legalized by the US Supreme Court in a 5-4 ruling. As a result, the outcome of American elections can be influenced by the activities of Super PACs who could be super-rich individuals. They can legally solicit and spend unlimited sums of money for political candidates of their choices for their election campaigns. That is equivalent to that the "money is speech" equation was legally acknowledged.

Hong What were the maladministration cases of the Clinton administration?

Kim I can identify two. First, the Clinton administration approved the repeal of the Glass-

Steagall Act—which was about effectively separating commercial banking from investment banking—and turned the entire banking and financing industry into an investment business. Secondly, the Clinton administration let China into the World Trade Organization (WTO) and dealt a critical blow to the US manufacturing industry as the consequence.

Hong In the first case you mentioned, you said it was his maladministration. But didn't it bring a windfall of wealth to American financial institutions, even though it brought about financial crisis in Asia, and Asian countries like Thailand, Malaysia, Indonesia and Korea had to suffer the consequences?

Kim But as time passed, the greed of the financial industry and their continuous speculative moves blew up into the financial crisis that hit America in 2008 and destroyed the American middle class.

Hong The destruction of the American middle class was such a shame, considering how in the 19th century, a prominent French sociologist had highly praised America as the country with "a classless middle-class society." Can you explain how China's membership in the WTO contributed to the destruction of the American manufacturing industry?

Kim When China became an official member of the WTO, China was a country with 1.4 billion population, and the workers had a high educational level and they were familiar with the strict disciplines of Communism. Chinese per capita income was about $1,000, which was about one-fortieth of that of Americans. Given that, it was a matter-of-course that the American manufacturing industry was hit hard by their Chinese counterpart.

Hong How did American political circles accept the fact that it was going to deal a fatal blow to the American manufacturing industry?

Kim It was quite possible under the plutocracy, because from the perspectives of the American super rich, China may have looked like a massive market for the future that would bring more wealth to them.

●●●

Hong There is a term that comes to my mind with regards to the Asian financial crisis. I've heard that people called the Asian leaders who went through that crisis "the Class of '98," am I correct? Since then Asian leaders made trading surplus and foreign reserves their top priority policies.

Kim You are correct. Leaders of the four Asian countries were called "the class of '98." Simply speaking, the dollar reserves these four Asian countries had been working so hard to save were swept away by the waves of speculative capital rushing in from other countries. To make things worse, they were left with enormous national debts in the wake of the crisis.

Hong How did the four Asian countries pull through

the crisis and survive?

Kim They were able to make forays into US markets thanks to the falling exchange rate and wages. Ironic as it may sound, it turned out that it was the US speculative capital that dealt a crushing blow to the US manufacturing industry.

Hong Where did the US speculative capital turn to after exploiting the wealth of those four Asian countries?

Kim It returned to the US mainland and shook down the middle class by preying on home equity, which in principle was the basis for the middle-class, and ultimately created the financial crisis in 2008.

Hong Are those responsible for the crisis in jail now?

Kim Far from it. As of now, they became the plutocrats who are leading the plutocracy.

Hong Who could be their next target?

Kim They might think China is their next target, but that is never going to happen. China has a non-market economy system under which its 1.4 billion population is under the dictatorship of a single communist party. The predatory lending which the American capitalists had used, ultimately causing the financial crises in Asia and America, will work only in a market economy system.

Hong How would you define predatory lending?

Kim It is about lending to those who will not be able to pay back and then foreclose their mortgages when their loans become delinquent. Simply put, it is the same as lending offered by crooked loan sharks, only on much bigger scales.

BUSH'S OIL-INDUSTRIAL COMPLEX STARTS THE IRAQ WAR

Kim The terms of Clinton (1993-2001) and George W. Bush (2001-2009) are almost overlapping with the terms of Kim Young-sam (1993-1998), Kim Dae-jung (1998-2003) and Roh Moo-hyun (2003-2008), because in Korea, presidency is limited to a single five-year term.

Hong I will talk about the accomplishments of these three Korean presidents if you will tell me about Bush first.

Kim Bush invaded Iraq in March 2003 claiming that Iraq possessed and refused to give up their weapons of mass destruction (WMDs)—which did not even exist—after warning about the invasion at a press conference in January the same year. A few months later on May 2, Bush proclaimed victory in Iraq aboard U.S. aircraft carrier Lincoln. But his proclaimed victory was no more than a hollow one.

Hong Why was that?

Kim It was a war against a foe that was no match for the US to begin with. Considering the difference in the military powers of the two countries, it was closer to the US reprimanding Iraq instead of a war. Besides, even though the US troops should have withdrawn immediately after the intended reprimand, they remained stationed in Iraq for close to ten years, playing the role of the police within Iraq.

Hong It reminds me of the atrocities committed by the Crusaders after they seized Jerusalem in the 11th century. A historian wrote, "One day in June 1099, rivers of blood flowed through the streets and even covered the horses' hooves galloping the streets of Jerusalem. The massacre of Muslims was terrifying."

Kim America was left with deep moral wounds not to mention the pain of significant economic damage. One economist termed the Iraq war as "the three trillion-dollar war."

Hong I have a question. If there was such a big difference in the military power, America could have achieved its objective through diplomatic channels. Why did American have to start a war instead?

Kim Avoiding war should absolutely be the mission of diplomacy. But this war was a collaboration between the MIC and another powerful body called the oil-industrial complex and should be understood as a case where the process of democracy was overpowered by their power.

Hong Isn't oil not directly related any longer to US national security since advanced shale gas technology made the United States become an oil exporting country? It's truly amazing when you think about it, because it's a case where yesterday's biggest oil importer became today's oil exporter.

Kim That's how abominable a technology revolution can be. Geopolitically speaking, it instantaneously changed the dynamics of international politics. Now, from a military point of view, the Middle East is not a very important region to America.

Hong I hope that the destruction of the Middle Eastern countries will be stopped now. They've suffered far too long already.

Kim The destruction of war won't come to a stop that easily, because there are religious issues involved as well, not to mention numerous countries that are depending on oil coming from the Middle East.

Hong If the importance of the oil-industrial complex diminishes, will a similar complex emerge?

Kim Probably. The next candidate is what we call 16 rare earth elements (REEs), even though their impact might not be as powerful as oil.

Hong Why are they so important?

Kim Because in the future, the winner of the

international competition will be determined by their competitiveness in three areas: chip design, robotics and artificial intelligence. Those rare-earth elements are absolutely necessary materials for these three fields.

Hong Is it true that China and North Korea make up most of the economically feasible deposits of REEs?

Kim As of today, China is known to have the world's largest reserves of economically feasible REEs. China is in fact producing close to 90% of the world supply. North Korea comes in second in terms of its reserves, but their qualities are far superior to those of China.

Hong Where does America come in this?

Kim US deposits are insignificant. Americans tried to refine their REE deposits, but their efforts failed because of their low quality. So, there are people who believe that in this currently on-going trade wars, the last card China could play is to ban the export of their REEs—even though it won't be an easy decision to make for China since the ban will be equivalent to declaring a war.

Hong That reminds me of something. One of North Korea's key intelligence officers had a meeting with Trump at the White House, and when he was leaving after the meeting was over, Trump personally accompanied him all the way to his car to see him off. And there is something else I remember. Trump sent executives of mining and agricultural companies to North Korea, which marked the first time the US sent American businessmen to North Korea.

Kim You made a keen observation. Trump's exceptional way of seeing off a North Korean delegate and sending executives from the US mining industry to North Korea should be understood as having a lot to do with North Korea's REEs. That's how important REEs are to America. Perhaps that's the reason Trump even proclaimed, "We fell in love," in which "we" meant Trump himself and Kim Jong-un.

Hong What was the reason executives of the agricultural industry were sent to the North?

Kim First, because sending executives from the mining industry alone would make their true intention too obvious, and second, because the US government could convince North Korea that they could improve North Korea's agricultural productivity.

Hong I can almost picture Trump secretly grinding an axe for North Korea's REEs. By the way, I wonder what ultimate solution Americans were thinking of regarding North Korea.

Kim They were attempting to kill three birds with one stone: contain China, solve North Korea's nuclear program issue, and solve the U.S.'s REEs problem. To tell from the perspective of South Korea, it needs to help America to take the lead in solving the REEs problem.

Hong Why is that?

Kim When China declared "Made in China 2025", its first target was Korea. If China gets what it wants, Korea will lose its competitiveness in advanced technology and become just a peripheral tributary state of China.

Hong How can Korea help the US with regard to the REEs problem?

Kim I remember an academic paper written by a pro-North American scholar when North Korea was under the rule of Kim Jong-il, the current leader's father. The key point of the paper was about making North Korea a monarchy similar to that of Thailand. The royal family of Thailand has political power and it also owns a significant part of the national wealth.

Hong It is an amazing suggestion. I wonder if that's what Trump is aiming for. He might be thinking of handling the North's royal family of Kim in the same way America did with King Faisal of Saudi Arabia. You know, trying to grab the upper hand on REEs now, like they did with the Saudis' petroleum back then. Going so far as to degrade himself by uttering such sugar-coated words as "We fell in love" with Kim Jong-un.... He's such an incredible leader.

Kim There was a very interesting point in that paper. It was about Kim Jong-il's daughter. In the paper, the author argued she could be a good candidate for Kim Jong-il's close aide and even his successor, since she is smart and studied economics, if by any chance Kim Jong-il's regime becomes similar to the monarchy of Thailand. In fact, that daughter is currently a close aide to her brother, Kim Jong-un now.

Hong The whole scenario sounds like fiction to me.... Indeed, there is a saying that "fiction is the lie through which we tell the truth."

ACCOMPLISHMENTS OF THE KIM YOUNG-SAM, KIM DAE-JUNG AND ROH MOO-HYUN ADMINISTRATIONS

Kim Clinton and Bush the son's terms covered 16 years from 1993 to 2009. As I mentioned previously, neither of the two leaders left any notable achievements during their presidencies. What about Korea during that period?

Hong President Kim Young-sam (1993-1998) was the first president without a military background since 1961 and he left several achievements. Firstly, he disbanded an unofficial private group of military officers and effectively prevented military power from getting involved in politics. His second achievement was an anti-corruption campaign, in which he introduced a real-name financial system and also required all government and military officials to register their assets to eradicate corruption that was rampant in our society. But he left a scar on his political career because his failed economic policy forced Korea to accept a bailout deal from the International Monetary Fund (IMF). One could say it was proof that he was not a ready-for-president material.

Kim Then came the era of Kim Dae-jung (1998-2003), who was ready to be president, and Korea was able to overcome the crisis. What other accomplishments did he leave during his presidency other than recovery of the Korean economy from IMF crisis?

Hong His other accomplishments include improved South-North relations, and in economy, they include the development of the IT industry and the modernization of finance and telecommunication industries. It was during his presidency that Korea laid the groundwork for the world's fastest Internet network. It was not a coincidence that Samsung Electronics could rank number one in global smartphone market shares.

Kim Next came the Roh Moo-hyun administration (2003-2008). His foremost accomplishment should be the free trade agreement (FTA) between Korea and the US.

Hong No question about it. One cannot talk about Roh Moo-hyun's accomplishments without mentioning the KOR-US FTA. It was something that would have been difficult to accomplish even under military dictatorship because of the intense protests by farmers and people from Korean movie industry.

Kim The determining reason the KOR-US FTA was approved by the US Congress was the fact that a friendly relationship with Korea was important for US national security. What are the rest of his accomplishments?

Hong His other accomplishments include the construction of a US military base in Pyeongtaek. When we look back from today's perspective, we realize it has been a critical key to the security of Korea and even to the stability of Northeast Asia as a whole. His other accomplishments are the introduction of the concept of administrative capital and ending a back-scratching collusion between politicians and *chaebol*s. In short, it was a move comparable to taking the first step to eradicate corruption in political circles.

Kim Aren't you going overboard with your praise of Korean leaders when I've been critical about their counterpart American leaders?

Hong But we have clear numbers that attest to the difference of two leaderships. Even if we compare situations post-1980s alone, the United States has been accumulating national debt until the amount of debt reached a scale unprecedented in their history, while Korea has been....

Kim Korea has been experiencing human rights violations and extreme political conflicts, hasn't it?

Hong It is true. The democratization uprising that took place on May 18,1980 in Gwangju left a disgraceful mark in our history. However, according to recent statistics released by the United Nations, Korea's GDP ranked 28th in the world as of 1980, but it jumped the rank to take the 11th place in the world in 2017. When considering the growth rate for the period of 1980-2017, Korea ranked the top of the world by far, according to the statistics, released by U.N..

Kim What exactly does that mean?

Hong It means that Korea's leaders have been far better than any other country's leaders in the world during the span of 38 years from 1980 to 2017. However, among the presidents who were in office during this period, four presidents were sent to jail after leaving office, one committed suicide, and two of them are currently imprisoned.

Kim Wasn't the leadership of President Park Chung-hee, who led Korea for 18 years beginning from 1961, superior even compared to those Korean presidents who came to office after 1980?

Hong It was Park Chung-hee who transformed Korea from one of the world's poorest countries into the world's 28th biggest economic power. There is not a comparable case throughout world history. Nonetheless, in 2017, the printing of a stamp in commemoration of the centenary anniversary of his birth was rejected by the related government agency.

Kim Why are Koreans so hard-hearted about their leaders?

Hong I do not know the fundamental reason... but I think Koreans definitely need to reflect on this regretful situation.

OBAMA, THE PUPPET OF PLUTOCRATS, ACCOMPLISHMENTS OF LEE MYUNG-BAK AND PARK GEUN-HYE

Hong Next comes the Obama administration (2009-2017), majority of which overlaps the Lee Myung-bak (2008-2013) and Park Geun-hye (2013-2017) administrations in Korea.

Kim Obama stepped into the presidential race two years after he became a senator, and two years later, he was elected as the first black president at the age of 48. You could say that he didn't have much job experience, because two years of being a US senator was the only real job experience he had.

Hong It is amazing that a 48-year old non-white man

with such a short job experience was elected president of the United States and became the leader of the free world.

Kim But there are two things that ended up becoming the yokes that bound him. One was the Nobel Peace Prize that he was awarded early in his presidency, and the other is the fact that plutocrats accounted for the majority of the big contributors to his election campaign (the total amount of his campaign contributions exceeded $1 billion for the first time in American history).

Hong Why are you saying they were the yokes that bound him?

Kim Nobel Peace Prize incapacitated Obama as the commander-in-chief. For example, China broke its original promise and installed military facilities on its artificially created Spratly Islands, but Obama remained helpless to do any concrete action to dismantle the military facilities.

Hong How did the massive campaign contributions bound him like a yoke?

Kim Plutocrats started the financial crisis in 2008,

during which process they destroyed the American middle class and burdened the US government with an astronomical amount of national debt. Yet, none of those plutocrats were sent to jail. According to the former French IMF chief, those plutocrats were ready to return at least half of their illicit profits in order to avoid going to jail at the time.

Hong Simply put, you mean Obama was the puppet of the plutocrats. When you think about it, I can imagine how contemptuous the Chinese leaders must have been of the American leaders.

Kim Then something happened during the Obama administration that added another reason for Chinese leaders to disdain American leaders. It was the super PAC, which became legalized by the US Supreme Court ruling in 2015. With this court decision, any company in the United States could put out unlimited advertisements to support an election candidate of their choice. That means, plutocrats found a legitimate way to control politicians.

Hong It is a case where democracy was driven out by plutocracy.

Kim Exactly. So, that's how China became so audacious. Subsequently in 2015, China launched the state-led industrial policy known as "Made in China 2025," which you cannot comprehend even with common sense. This plan should have been treated as a national top-secret paper, but China ended up publicly declaring it, giving good cause for Western advanced countries around the world to unite and raise their guard against China as one. This unity was realized only after Trump presidency.

Hong I see the point. Obama's indecisive attitude unintentionally dug a trap for China to be audacious enough to make a blunder and push China to fall into the trap by way of proclaiming "Made in China 2025". Politics and diplomacies are indeed an unpredictable and a complicated game.... Well, then, shall we set Obama aside and start talking about his contemporary Korean leaders?

Kim All right. However, two of those Korean leaders were incarcerated as of the end of 2018. I believe that in the history of mankind, there has never been another case in which two preceding presidents are locked up in prison. Given the unusual circumstance of the case, please try to be more generous when you give me your account of the two former presidents' accomplishments.

Hong After being sworn into office, President Lee Myung-bak's first mission was to prevent the US-originated financial crisis from spilling over to Korea in 2008. Ultimately, he prevented it successfully, and he also made a remarkable achievement in improving the environments in local communities as the result of so-called 'Quantitative Easing' fund his administration spent for social overhead capital for the purpose of the prevention.

Kim Didn't he host the G20 conference in Seoul as well?

Hong Yes, he did host the 5th G20 conference in 2010. Korea was the first to host the conference other than countries that belong to G8 (G6 plus Canada and Russia). That event in Seoul definitely contributed to the elevation of Korea's status in the international community. The internationally acclaimed overhaul of the public transportation system that covers metropolitan Seoul area is another accomplishment of Lee Myung-bak in his capacity as Seoul city mayor (2002-2006) and then the president.

Kim I've heard that there are lots of controversies over Lee Myung-bak administration's four-river refurbishment project.

Hong No matter who says what about it, there might come a day when all Korean people will appreciate the four-river refurbishment project for having made Korea a country free from the risk of flood and drought.

Kim Many would criticize you for overrating Lee's accomplishments.... Let's leave that subject now and I want to ask you to tell me about the accomplishments made by Park Geun-hye (2013-2017) who was impeached and had to leave office about one year before her term was over.

Hong President Park disbanded a pro-North Korean political party and prosecuted the party leader on charges including the conspiracy to overthrow the nation. It can be acknowledged as her accomplishment because it stopped the proliferation of the ideology that supported the North's one-party dictatorship. Her other accomplishment that cannot be missed is the enforcement of a broad anti-corruption bill (Kim Young-ran law), which laid the foundation for a more transparent Korean society. She also reformed the National Pension Act.

Kim As far as I know, it was also Park Geun-hye who made the decision on the deployment of THAAD on the Korean peninsula, wasn't it? Even though I'm not so sure if that was a wise decision.

Hong It may be safe to say that it was her accomplishment considering how China reacted to her decision. China's harsh reaction to the deployment of THAAD on the Korean Peninsula can be safely construed as a proof that it was what Korea really needed. The more meaningful gain from the THAAD controversy was that it revealed China's hidden view of Korea. It was that China still kept a traditional view of Korea as no more than "a small state at the edge of China that should pay tribute to them."

Part II

KOREA BRANCHING OUT TO THE WORLD, WHERE IS AMERICA HEADED IN THE TRUMP ERA?: 2017-2018

TRUMP DECLARES "AMERICA FIRST"

Kim Now we have moved past the era of Obama and arrived at the era of Trump who was sworn into office in January 2017. I think there is so much to talk about. He's been in office for about two years, but so many things have happened already.

Hong Let me ask you a straightforward question. Is Trump a racist?

Kim During the presidential race in 2016 and midterm elections in 2018, Trump used two slogans: Make America Great Again, and America First. It is true that Trump has been constantly and implicitly attacked and accused by rival groups for being a racist, probably because his main political base is white middle-class. But Trump himself strongly denies that allegation.

Hong Is Trump anti-Semitic?

Kim It is true that he has been suspected of being anti-Semitic because he's been attacking and accusing conventional mass media outlets—which are mostly dominated by wealthy Jews—branding them "fake news", and he's been also accusing the financial industry—which is also dominated by Jewish people—for destroying the middle class. But his son-in-law is Jewish, and his daughter converted to Judaism.

Hong How did he attack them?

Kim In his inaugural speech, there was a part that was apparently written by Trump himself. It read: "The wealth of our middle class has been ripped from their homes and then redistributed across the entire world."

Hong You mean he believes that it is a group of financial businessmen, the majority of whom are Jewish, that was doing the "redistribution" that he mentioned in his inaugural speech.

Kim That's right.

Hong Why do you think so?

Kim That particular phrase was removed from Trump's inaugural address on most websites controlled by Jewish groups. That shows how the Jewish people took the sentence as Trump targeting them.

Hong It makes me realize the power of the Jewish group in this era of the Internet. It's possible those who dominate social media might be able to unleash even more power than those who dominate the previously powerful news media.

Kim It is a challenge we need to find a solution for when looking to the future. At any rate, Trump has been actively denying it whenever he is accused of being anti-Semitic, but he could not easily escape the accusation. However, there is one thing that is certain: He is a faithful follower of the evangelical church and a descendant of immigrants who came from Germany where Martin Luther began the Protestant Reformation.

Hong What does that signify?

Kim He might not be able to forsake his belief that Protestantism should be the religion that dominates American minds. So, Trump's cabinet meetings begin with a prayer. In this sense, it is inevitable for his administration to have a confrontational relationship with Jewish intellectuals who advocate "separation of state and religion."

Hong Why are the Jewish people advocating that?

Kim It is because it is not an overstatement to say that the Jewish people's history of suffering unfolded within the frame where church and state were not separated.

WAR BETWEEN TRUMP AND FAKE NEWS, AND CHINA'S MISCALCULATION

Hong Another very distinctive mark of the Trump administration is their extremely confrontational relations with the majority of the mainstream news media outlets. In a tweet posted on his Twitter account on February 17, 2017, 1:00 am, Trump attacked The New York Times, NBC, ABC, CBS, and CNN by branding them as enemies of the state. Those are news media outlets that represent America.... Will Trump be able to survive this, ultimately?

Kim I think that at this point, nobody can predict who will win in this collision between Trump and "the fake news" as Trump has branded it.

Hong What does "win" mean in this case?

Kim For the news media, it means impeaching Trump, and for Trump, it means making the news media lose its credibility.

Hong Whoever comes out as the winner, will it be any help to America or even to the world?

Kim Nobody can give you a clear answer to that question. But one thing is sure. Whoever comes out of it as the winner, it will bring about dramatic changes in the political spectrum of America as well as of the world.

Hong What about from the perspective of Korea?

Kim From the perspective of Korea, Trump has to win in this war.

Hong Why is that?

Kim If Trump loses his war, it is impossible to expect Trump to be succeeded by another president who has the same guts to knock down the audacious Chinese. Korea succeeded in becoming an advanced country with the support of its advanced technologies such as the semiconductor, but if that happens, there is no doubt that Korea will lose those technologies to China as well as its hard-earned status of being an advanced country. There is even a possibility that we will repeat history and Korea becomes a country at the edge that has to pay tribute to China.

Hong Didn't China demonstrate its ultimate arrogance in 2015 when it revealed its ambition to debase even the United States into just a country that supplies agricultural products such as soybeans that China consumes in large quantities, even though military-related and some highly-advanced technologies and industries should be exceptions?

Kim That's right. The "Made in China 2025" that China had publicly declared in 2015 was a type of manifesto, or the blueprint of their future. China has suffered retaliation by Trump in many ways beginning in late 2018 because of this declaration. That is the perfect example of "reaping the fruits of one's actions", because it was the outcome of

China's foolishness, arrogance, and impatience.

Hong At the same time, isn't it also true that Trump elevated himself to become the leader of the world by winning the support of East Asian countries as well as advanced Western countries with his bold actions against China?

Kim That is a good point. Advanced Western countries were not able to handle China with their own power alone, but they were able to join and unite into a firm power after Trump stepped out to the front. Eventually, the stupidity of China ended up helping Trump to leap into the prominent status of a leader comparable to the status of Eisenhower who served as the Supreme Commander of the Allied Expeditionary Forces during World War II—in Trump's case, as the supreme commander in the battle between a non-market economy and market economy.

Hong How could China be so stupid?

Kim Throughout the history of China, she has invariably demonstrated the qualifications worthy of a great power. Whether you look back at Chinese history that goes far back to ancient days, or even only the post-Deng Xiaoping history of China, there have never been Chinese leaders who demonstrated the stupidity that China has shown in its "Made in China 2025."

Hong True, there has never been any stupidity of that magnitude. Rather, the wisdom of Taizong of the Tang Dynasty who was willing to accept and embrace Christianity and Islam religions as early as in the 7th century is an epitome of China's proud history of wisdom. Even in her modern history, the flexible leadership of Deng Xiaoping —who famously said, "It doesn't matter whether a cat is black or white, as long as it catches mice."—received world-wide acknowledgement of his outstanding leadership during the process of his opening up policy, despite his blemishes of brutal crackdown on the Tiananmen Square protests. So, what made the current Chinese leaders so stupid?

Kim I don't quite understand it either. There is one explanation that comes to my mind, even though it might not sound very convincing. It seems to me that Chinese economists who are serving Chinese leaders as their advisers are so intimidated by Western intellectuals—perhaps without even realizing it themselves—that they have been following their opinions only. Among them, there is one particular intellectual who has been advising the Chinese government for almost 25 years since the early 1990s.

Hong Who is that?

Kim He is the winner of the 2001 Nobel prize in economics. He discredited Trump by claiming that he belongs to minority, not majority of American supporters because he received less popular votes than Clinton in the 2016 presidential race. He has also continuously highlighted and magnified the possibility of Trump's impeachment.

●●●

Hong Don't you think the possibility is thin for this collision between Trump and the mainstream news media outlets to come to an end any time soon?

Kim From the perspective of mainstream news media outlets, it would be admitting that they are generating fake news and thus, cannot remain credible sources if they accept the incumbent president who publicly attacks them for generating fake news whenever he has a chance. Therefore, they can't afford to raise a white flag.

Hong Isn't it also true in Trump's position? Even though he is getting the help of smaller friendly media, he has no other choice but to utilize Twitter as his main weapon to fight against the hostile, powerful media in order to maintain the base of his supporters necessary to play the role as president.

Kim You are right. Therefore, we should hold off making a final conclusion until the 2020 presidential election. If Trump is re-elected, Trump will become more generous to the mass media because he is proven to have reliable support groups, and the mass media will change the tone of their editorials to conform to the direction of public opinion.

Hong It is actually a little absurd for the president of the world's strongest super power to fight against the news media of his own country through Twitter for 4 years until 2020. But since it is the outcome of advanced Internet technology, perhaps we can just accept it as a by-product that has more of a positive side than a negative side.

Kim What is the positive side of it?

Hong One good example of its positive side is that increasing use of social media has effectuated the declining risk of opinion manufacturing by the press, which had raised concerns in the past.

Kim I guess you are right. Anyway, the confrontation of the two parties can eventually prove to be a blessing in disguise for both of them. Wouldn't the mass media become more faithful to public opinion rather than trying to manufacture public opinion, and the President be more careful not to become despotic or abuse his power since hard-bitten hostiles are keeping an eye on him?

Hong A German philosopher once defined human nature as "the will to power." If this definition is true, humans will never cease their efforts to gain power. People's mentality in a modern society that constantly seeks wealth is the consequence of an unreasonable coupling effect of wealth and power in modern society, especially of plutocratic tendencies.

Hong What would happen if this coupling of wealth and power continue?

Kim The wealth of the so-called "0.1%" will continue to increase, while the gap between the rich and the poor grows bigger until it gives rise to such mass movements as "Occupy Wall Street" and brings extreme chaos to society. When the US was hit by the financial crisis in 2008, such public movements could be managed because the mainstream press stepped out to put them under control. But the press will not be able to exercise the same influential power that it exerted during the financial crisis, now that it is branded as "fake news", evidenced by the fact that most of their predictions of the last U.S. presidential election turned out to be wrong. The "Yellow Vest" protest, which began in Paris, France at the end of 2018, is not going to die out that easily exactly for this reason: people distrust the mainstream media.

Hong Do you think there is any solution?

Kim In fact, there is a simple solution. It is to separate thoroughly industrial and financial capital from the media capital. Korea has been doing it for some time. By doing so, the media can truly maintain editorial independence; thus can the media put a restraint on the powerful while protecting the powerless. Only then can we ensure the stability of society.

Hong Do you think the media can sustain and survive on its own financially without the infusion of blood from the industrial capital?

Kim As far as the operational finance issue is concerned, it will be able to solve the problem purely with voluntary donations provided by wealthy public-minded individuals, as long as it can maintain editorial independence.

THE WAR BETWEEN TRUMP AND MAINSTREAM MEDIA: WHO WILL BE THE WINNER?

Kim It was not long after Trump took office and started his presidency that a Hungarian-Jewish businessman who is considered the Godfather of hedge funds and runs an ideology research organization called Open Society appeared on a CNN TV program and attacked US President Trump, saying, "He is a fraud and a con man."

Hong It is amazing. It can only happen in America. But for what purpose did he publicly attack him using such strong words?

Kim He was openly expressing his commitment to bring down the president through impeachment by using all the resources he had, while at the same time declaring his confidence that the impeachment would be done to the world.

Hong How can a mere businessman who immigrated from Hungary have such a confidence? It is beyond my understanding.

Kim His confidence must emanate from the mainstream media circle that he's been empowering with his wealth and a network of his secret confidantes within the bureaucrat society called the Deep State, in particular within the circle of law enforcement organizations such as the FBI.

Hong There is no way that Trump will fail to get the message about the impeachment, is there? And also that this businessman's confidence is founded upon his powerful influence over the mainstream media.

Kim Of course, he became fully aware of all that. That's the reason Trump has been attacking the mainstream media branding them fake news despite all kinds of risks.

Hong There is something I'm really curious about. What do you think is the main reason Jewish people came to dominate almost all mainstream media outlets?

Kim I can think of several reasons, with two of them particularly convincing. One of the reasons must be that Jewish people preferred the press as the means to have their voices heard because the entire Jewish population of the world stands at only about 20 million. Another reason is that Jewish people are born with superior linguistic ability and writing skills. Anybody who has read the Old Testament of the Bible, especially the Ecclesiastes, Psalms, and Proverbs parts of the Old Testament, will agree with that.

Hong Pardon me for this absurd question but let me ask straightforwardly. Why did Trump turn the mainstream media into his enemy and burn the bridge by branding them "fake news", even though he fully knew that he needed their support to do his job as the president smoothly. Did he think he had a chance to win outright over them?

Kim There was a reason for that. Besides a few mainstream media outlets that were favorable to him, he probably believed in the efficacy of Twitter that he had frequently used during his election campaign. Even after he became the president he continued tweeting on Twitter about both domestic and international affairs in the early morning hours just as he had done during the election campaign. Then the mainstream news media outlets wrote articles for morning news hours based on his tweets, which is rather comical and which could only happen in the era of social media. The interesting thing is that since then, leaders of other advanced Western countries followed his suit and became patronizing users of social media.

Hong But I wonder if the hedge fund mogul's attack on the incumbent president—calling him "a fraud and a con man"—can be interpreted in a different way. For example, maybe it was his counterattack against the attack—or defense against an attack initiated by Trump by way of his inauguration address.

Kim What do you mean by Trump's attack?

Hong You quoted to me a sentence of Trump's inauguration address. Don't you think it was his first attack, more like a declaration of war? Can you quote that part again?

Kim He said, "The wealth of our middle class has been ripped from their homes and then redistributed across the entire world." This part must have been written by Trump himself.

Hong I think we need answers to "when and how" the wealth of America's middle class has been ripped and redistributed.

Kim As to your question about "when?" I can tell you it happened three times. The first time it happened was during the Asian financial crisis in 1997, and the second time was when China joined WTO in 2001. And the third was when the problematic subprime mortgage loans blew up into a financial crisis in America in 2008.

Hong I guess it is not easy to answer about "how?".

Kim Actually, it is. The answer is actually simple

and clear. All three crises eventually resulted in the sacrifices of the American middle class. On the other hand, for your reference, American financiers profited from all three crises.

Hong How did the American middle class become the victims of all three crises?

Kim In the first case of the Asian financial crisis, the skyrocketing exchange rates in countries that were hit by the crisis resulted in their increased competitiveness in exports to the United States because of depreciation of their currencies. The consequence was that the employment rate among the American middle class went down. In the case of China's admission to WTO, it made China the factory for manufacturers of the world because China boasted low wages and high educational level of workers. That in turn brought about the closing of numerous factories in America. In the third case of the US-originated financial crisis, it resulted in the foreclosures of many homes of the American middle class, which used to constitute an important social foundation.

So, it brought about the collapse of the American middle class, which is considered as the safety net of society.

Hong I see. Then, can I summarize the development of collision between Trump and the mainstream media like this?

"Trump initiated an attack by pointing out the public enemies of the American middle class in his inaugural address, and those who were pointed out made a counterattack by mobilizing the mass media that were under their influence. In response, Trump has been launching attacks on them whenever he has a chance, accusing the mass media which boasts a long tradition and reputation as being "fake news"."

Kim It seems a good summary.

Hong Who do you think will be the final winner?

Kim They are both in a position where they cannot back down, because one is a president elected by the people and the other is a self-proclaimed and also commonly acknowledged cornerstone of democracy. If you want to bring down the president elected by the people, you need to go through the impeachment process. But if the Congress pushes forward with impeaching him when he did not commit any crime that amounts to a treasonous act, Trump supporters are likely to rebel against it and even start a violent revolt. And the mass media is also in a situation where it cannot surrender unconditionally either.

Hong The standoff should come to an end one way or another, though. You cannot let this confrontational situation linger on for the rest of the President's term, can you?

Kim In the end, it will be determined by the President's approval rating, and the critical factors that determine approval rating are his performance as President, particularly his performance on the economy. The famous quote that goes "It's the economy, stupid" might apply in this case.

A LOOK INTO THE REALITY OF AMERICAN MAINSTREAM MEDIA

Hong Didn't Trump lose to the Democratic candidate in the 2016 presidential election in a popular vote? Considering that, do you think he has a chance to be re-elected in the 2020 presidential election?

Kim I would say he is sure to be reelected. Trump has a strong base of support from German-Americans among his white middle-class supporters. That is the strength of Trump.

Hong How strong is the German-American group's power?

Kim Otto von Bismark, a statesman who dominated a united Germany for close to 20 years, once said,

"The most significant event of the 20th century will be the fact that the North Americans speak English." A subtle nuance hidden in his statement is that the United States could have decided to use German as its official language. The background of this statement is the waves of Germans who immigrated to the United States to escape the political instability of Germany and other European countries during the 19th century.

Hong Can you elaborate in specific numbers?

Kim According to statistics released in 2015, the number of German-American citizens in the United States is 46 million, which makes them the largest single ethnic group. It is followed by 38 million African-Americans, 34 million Mexican Americans, 33 million Irish-Americans and 24 million British Americans.

Hong Does the ethnic background matter significantly?

Kim There is a saying that blood is thicker than water. It seems that the ethnic background still cannot be ignored even though many years have passed since their immigration. There is an Academy award-winning actor who played one of the main roles in the movie Midnight Cowboy. He is a passionate supporter of Trump, a rare case in Hollywood, whose mother is a German descendent. He shed tears while mentioning Trump on a TV interview.

Hong What was the context of the interview?

Kim In the interview, the actor, who is close to his 80s now, said that when he asked an actress friend, "What do think of our man in Washington?" the friend put her hand over the left side of her chest and shed tears, exclaiming, "Oh, my God!"

Hong Germans being the descendants of Beethoven, I'm sure they tend to be easily emotional. What are their other characteristics?

Kim Germans take manufacturing very seriously. It is almost to a religious level. Maybe that is why Trump is so proud of his construction business. On the other hand, they have a tendency to look down upon the wealth built by financing activities.

Hong Then, what professions do the German-

Americans prefer?

Kim German-American citizens mostly live in inland cities, instead of coastal cities, and they mostly engage in agriculture and manufacturing fields. Germans have the belief that physical work, instead of financial or wholesale or retail work, represents truly valuable and even sacred forms of labor. Maybe their belief is influenced by Christian teaching.

Hong Are you implying that there is an ethnic group that has a tendency that is the opposite of the Germans?

Kim There is an ethnic group that demonstrates a tendency that is completely the opposite of that of the German-Americans. It is the Jewish-American group that owns the majority of American mass media, which Trump has been constantly attacking as "fake news" whenever he has a chance since he was elected the president.

Hong It is hard to imagine that happening in Korea where the president of a country openly and publicly attacks prominent news media outlets that have been the cornerstone of democracy, derogatorily calling them "the fake news".

Kim At any rate, unlike German-Americans, the Jewish-Americans are mostly concentrated in coastal states such as New York, California, and Florida. While the German-Americans account for the largest single ethnic group in America with its 46 million population, the number of Jewish-American citizens is only 5.4 million. However, since the number of Jews scattered all over the world is less than 20 million, America has the second largest number of Jews following Israel where the Jewish population is over 6 million.

Hong In that sense, one might even call America the second home of Jews. In America, which is their second home, Jews excel and stand out in fields of finance and arts including pop arts, as well as the high-techs(such as Google and Facebook), academics, journalism and law.

Kim Jews particularly stand out in legal professions. For example, three out of the nine Supreme Court

Justices in the US Supreme Court are Jews. That means Jews that account only for less than 2 percent of the entire population of the United States account for 33.3 percent of the Supreme Court justices. That speaks of their superiority as an ethnic group.

Hong Isn't their presence more apparent in journalism?

Kim Journalism is a field where Jews stand out just as much as they do in legal professions. In particular, the cable news network, which is a newly emerged field with the arrival of the Internet era, must have been a prey which Jewish capitalists could not ignore because it is a field with a particularly promising future.

Hong How about the conventional printed press?

Kim The conventional printed press has been on a downward spiral in the wake of the development of advanced broadcasting and telecommunication technology and is reaching out to wealthy investors to resolve its mounting deficit problem. Some of the good examples include the New York Times and the Washington Post. Others are trying to sell their newspaper companies at bargain prices or are left with no option other than closing their operations all together.

Hong Aren't the original owners of the New York Times and the Washington Post highly intellectual ideologist Jews who could be considered as direct descendants of the Jewish Karl Marx, the founder of communism? And aren't they the very people behind the American Exceptionalism that is identified as the highest virtue of America worthy of its world leadership status?

Kim But now, a massive industrial capital has swallowed up the capital of media that has a long tradition of serving as American society's fundamental backbone, thereby eroding the editorial independence of media until it went on a downward spiral and became subject to constant attack from the president who branded it as "fake news."

Hong Can you give me an example of industrial capital having swallowed up media capital?

Kim When the founder of Amazon took over the Washington Post for a mere $250 million, or less than 1% of his wealth, he took control of a paper with an amazing tradition and dignity. He publicly claimed that he would honor the editorial independence of the newspaper and not interfere with its operation, but that was just a hollow promise.

Hong I think Korea's long-standing legal separation of industrial and financial capital from media capital seems an excellent policy.

Kim I totally agree with you. The U.S. has to learn to pick up superior policies of other countries.

●●●

Hong I can think of another case in which Korea is doing a better job compared to the United States. It's income inequality. When you compare the Gini coefficient, which goes up when income inequality grows, the United States scores 45.0

and ranks 39th in the world, while Korea scores 35.7 and ranks 93rd in the world. Besides, the score of the United State is as of 2007 and Korea, 2016. While Korea fares well in terms of the income inequality because it ranks 93rd in the world, it is probable that American financial crisis of 2008 might have aggravated American income inequality level considerably.

Kim No question about it. During the 2016 presidential campaign, one progressive candidate said, "the wealth of the top 0.1% equals the total sum of wealth of the lower 90% of people."

Hong It is a shocking statement. What on earth is the main reason for this inequality?

Kim Simply put, the wealth of the top 0.1% can never become equal to the total sum of wealth of the lower 90%, unless plutocrats somehow control the press, politics, and bureaucrat society.

Hong I wonder exactly what kind of a group these plutocrats you mentioned really are.

AMERICAN PLUTOCRATS DESTROY THE AMERICAN MIDDLE CLASS

Kim It is the group that Trump publicly attacked in his inaugural speech in 2017 when he said, "The wealth of our middle class has been ripped from their homes and then redistributed across the entire world."

Hong Trump's accusation in his inaugural address must have been taken as a serious threat by the targeted group. I am curious about the identity of those who belong to the targeted group.

Kim They are the plutocrats that belong to the so-called "America's top 0.1%" who had been building wealth for 37 years since Reagan took office in 1980. The exact scale of the wealth that this 0.1% has accumulated is not revealed, but the gap between the rich and the poor has been constantly widening in America for the last 37 years.

Hong Is there a proof that the gap was widening?

Kim The US economic growth rate for those 37 years has been just 2-3%, but the income increase rate of the 0.1% is estimated to be 5-7% for the same period. That means, it is a numerically proven that wealth has been transferred from the 99.9% to the 0.1% at the annual rate of 2-4%. This theory also applies to other advanced Western European countries, such as England, France, and Italy due to the globalized financial system.

Hong What has been the top 0.1%'s annual return on their wealth?

Kim I estimate it to be around 7%. According to a complex mathematical formula, an annual return of 7% means the principle doubles every ten years. This theory is also called the Rule of Seventy. Applying this formula for 40-year period from 1980 to 2020 on 7% annual return, the amount of wealth doubles four times (2, 4, 8, 16) and becomes 16 times the original. For example, if you had $100 million in 1980, the amount will grow to $1.6 billion 40 years later in 2020.

Hong And that will make one a billionaire. Let me try some mental arithmetic here. Suppose there is a billionaire whose wealth is exactly $1 billion right now. If the annual growth rate is 7%, the billionaire will rake in about $200,000 every day, and the daily return besides the principal keeps accruing daily, rain or shine, throughout the year. In other words, a billionaire earns in a day more money with his principal of $1 billion than the entire annual income of an average American middle-class family.

Kim Exactly. This group of billionaires might have had a misconceived notion that they owned the world. The collapse of the former Soviet Union in 1991, the biggest threat in the Cold War era, and the weakening of labor unions in private sector since 1980 when Reagan took office might have instigated their misconception.

Hong What did they contribute to the world that they seemingly own?

Kim Instead of establishing new companies, they went on the hunt for companies through M&A, and they often made windfall profits either by cost cutting via restructuring or splitting up the companies that they hunted. For the most part, they recorded more than 7% annual return through these kinds of aggressive organizational shake-ups.

Hong I bet they constantly needed to hunt for new sources of income to maintain such a high return. I wonder how they did it.

Kim So, they turned their attention to two new markets: The Asian financial market that was forced to open beginning in the late 1990s, and the American home equity market which they started to infiltrate into, beginning in the early 2000s. As you are well aware, the first market that they had exploited resulted in the Asian financial crisis, and the second market, the financial crisis in the US.

Hong The victims of the first market were the people of Asian countries that went through the first financial crisis. The American middle-class homeowners who lost their houses in the wake of the American financial crisis were the victims of the second market. On the other hand this 0.1% did not suffer any damages themselves. Instead, they became financially stronger than before.

Kim You are right on.

Hong Who will be their next target? I'm sure it's not easy to find a target that can yield an annual return of 7%.

Kim Surprisingly, China did not sustain any damage throughout the two crises—the Asian financial crisis and the US financial crisis. Rather, China was able to grow comparatively stronger in the wake of those crises. China is maintaining about 7% annual economic growth rate, and that could make China their next target. But will China be an easy target?

Hong It won't be an easy target, because the Chinese communist party leaders must be well aware already of their intentions. China also has the experience of avoiding a financial crisis by thoroughly blocking American speculative capital from entering into Chinese financial markets during the Asian financial crisis. It was mostly thanks to totalitarian nature of Communist Chinese government.

Kim China might play innocent and accept the conspiracy of the top 0.1% if those who belong to the 0.1% demonstrate their influence over US politics and convince China that their influence could work in China's overall favor.

Hong The United States and China have already strained their relations while confronting each other over the current trade war, perhaps as a prelude to a hegemony war. Any kind of collaboration of the top 0.1% with China's Communist government will bring about antagonism domestically and internationally will distance these two countries further than they are now.

EMERGENCE OF THE WEALTH OF THE TOP 0.1% AND GLOBALISM

Hong There are people who connect the top 0.1% with Jews living in America. Why is that?

Kim Perhaps because, even though the population of Jews living in America is about 5.4 million, which accounts for only about 2 percent of the entire US population, there are many super rich Jews among them.

Hong Can you give me some examples that describe what kind of people Jews are?

Kim One example will be the character of Shylock in Shakespeare's the *Merchant of Venice* and his famous soliloquy in the book.

Hong I've read the *Merchants of Venice*, but I don't remember the soliloquy you are referring to. I'm curious what it was.

Kim It starts and ends like this, as far as I remember. It starts with "I am a Jew. Hath not a Jew eyes?" and it ends with "If you wrong us, do we not revenge? If we are like you in the rest, we will resemble you in that." Don't you feel how his heart is seething with the urge to revenge?

Hong All the Jews who lost their homeland and were living scattered throughout Europe under extreme duress around the 16th century would have felt the same urge. Don't you agree?

Kim On the outside, Shylock is the most parsimonious man but on the inside, he is an agonizing intellect with rich sensibility, as you can tell from his monologue. The sensibility of Jewish people might have been cultivated by the constant recitation of their sacred scriptures of Judaism and by their long history of suppressions.

Hong What if I say Rothschild is representing the former, and Karl Marx, the latter. What do you think?

Kim That's an interesting analogy. So, Rothschild family emerged as a financial dynasty in the European financial circles in the early 19th century, and Karl Marx with his followers presented to the world an alternative to Capitalism in the mid-19th century. However, Karl Marx's theory of communism was put into practice in the former Soviet Union in 1917, but it ended in a total failure when the former Soviet Union collapsed about 70 years later in 1991.

Hong What is the core point of Karl Marx's Communist theory?

Kim According to the *Communist Manifesto* that was published in 1847 by Marx and Engels, its essence is the abolition of private ownership and the dictatorship of the proletariat. But the abolition of private ownership eventually caused the collapse of the Soviet Union. A society without private ownership is bound to have neither competition nor individual freedom. And a society without competition makes people lazy and eventually poor, and a society that has no individual freedom is destined to see its leaders turning corrupt.

Hong What did "proletarian dictatorship" originally mean?

Kim Marx wanted a world order that transcended the concept of nation. His logic was that, if any nation was ruled by the proletariat mass, there will be no conflict among countries, and even the interest group called a nation itself can be eliminated. In truth, the organization that oppressed Jews was a nation, a Christian nation, in particular.

Hong In that sense, one can say that Marx's attempt made through Lenin ended up a complete failure with the fall of the former Soviet Union.

Kim You can say that. But the Jews' attempt to eliminate the concept of nation was not over yet. There was a new attempt beginning around 1993 (inauguration of Clinton), which was two years after the collapse of the former Soviet Union. This time, it was the Jewish capitalist group, instead of the intellectual group, that took action.

And that came to be known as the ideology of globalism.

Hong Does that mean both communism and globalism share the same essential goal? Then, I wonder what the goal is.

Kim The goal is accurately described in the French version of "The Internationale", which is a left-wing anthem. There is a part in the song that goes, "And end the vanity of nations. We have one earth to live on." This part makes it clear that the desire for communism is about getting rid of the concept of nation. It is because of the strong belief that a nation state is the cause of the suffering of the Jewish people.

Hong Is it true that Hitler once lamented that New York's Wall Street is occupied by Jewish people and so is Moscow's Red Square?

Kim I heard that too. That means that Jewish people can be both pragmatic idealists and idealistic pragmatists; neither a pure communist nor a shrewd financier.

Hong Anyway, Marx believed that the concept of nation

and the associated narrow-minded ideas such as patriotism and religious faith were the cause of war among nations and racial discrimination. Was it really the cause?

Kim Nobody has a clear answer to that question. But one thing is for sure. When you look back at the long Jewish history of suffering, you can understand their fear of nationalism. Even after the 13th century, most of the Christian countries in Europe had either deported Jewish people or committed atrocities against them. The people of European countries that persecuted Jewish people should have a guilty conscience about the history of cruelty against Jewish people committed by their ancestors.

Hong I've read that anti-Semitism tends to rise again lately in European countries instead of feeling guilty about their past oppressions of Jewish people. What is the reason?

Kim Jewish people who are enjoying financial superiority should try to understand non-Jewish people's feeling toward them and also try to be more humble. Only then will this animosity be restrained.

Hong On what grounds do you say that?

Kim Envy is a human nature. Envy can be defined in many ways, but to me, envy is a hatred you have toward a person who makes you feel inferior. The hatred that some people who belong to the lower than middle-class hold against Jewish people who are in a superior financial position is a natural manifestation of human nature. You cannot resist human nature, and even if you tried, your resistance will be futile. If you criticize that human nature itself, the hatred will be hidden inside and only grow stronger.

Hong So, what's the solution?

Kim A group that is the target of hatred should have patience and tolerance. Only through that process can hatred lose its sharp edges and be converted into admiration, which can be a source of motivation to catch up with the other party. It is a concept that is the opposite of hatred that gives you the urge to destroy the other party.

Hong The solution is that the rich's attitude toward one's wealth shall be a consolation to be free of money, not as a tool to intimidate other people. It won't be a difficult task because as Socrates said 24 centuries ago, it is a human nature to love what we have less and do not love what we have plenty.

THE POWER THAT MOVES AMERICAN SOCIETY: THE WEALTH OF JEWS

Kim There is something I'd like to know about Jews. I believe this question should be answered by a sociologist or a psychologist, or even a writer like you. Are the Jewish people born with a certain trait that makes them particularly obsessive about money?

Hong Well… As you know, the Christian Bible includes the Old Testament, which is largely the Hebrew Bible of Judaism. In terms of volume, the Old Testament accounts for more than two-thirds of the Bible. The Pentateuch refers to the first five books of the Bible that starts with Genesis.

Kim The Old Testament and the New Testament have many contradictory phrases between the two, don't they? For example, the part that goes "an eye for an eye and a tooth for a tooth" in the Old Testament is contradictory to "if anyone slaps you on the right cheek, turn to him the other" in the New Testament, which advocates forgiveness rather than vengeance.

Hong There are differences not just about vengeance, but also about wealth as well. For example, the following verse appears in the Book of Ecclesiastes, which is known to be the work of Solomon;

> "A feast is made for laughter, and wine makes life merry, but money is the answer for everything." (Ecclesiastes 10:19)

On the contrary, the following verses appear in the Book of Luke:

> "Blessed are the poor, for yours is the kingdom

of God." (Luke 6:20)

……

"But woe to you who are rich, for you have already received your comfort." (Luke 6:24)

The New Testament records the words of Jesus who was critical about those who were rich and who loved the poor.

Kim The part that says "money is the answer for everything" is quite shocking to me. Particularly because the phrase was preceded by two obvious benefits of wine and a feast.

Hong We can assume that the last part about money left a significant influence on the mentality of Jews.

Kim How? And through what process?

Hong There is a feast of the Jews called the "feast of tents" that commemorates the days Moses spent in the wilderness. In modern times, children usually spend a short time camping in the open air and then recite the Book of Ecclesiastes before concluding the feast. The part that children recite includes the same sentence, "money is the answer for everything."

Kim So, they are bound to be influenced by it since childhood. In some ways, Ecclesiastes is a very dangerous book.

Hong Truth is always dangerous, because for those who cannot handle the truth, it can always be harmful. Perhaps for that reason, it is said that Ecclesiastes is the least quoted book by preachers among all books of the Bible.

Kim Can you give me a few examples of people who can handle that kind of truth?

Hong They are mostly artists and scholars. Therefore, the contents of Ecclesiastes are often used in the titles or content of famous novels, movies, and songs. There are three to four that I can think of offhand.

Kim What are they?

Hong There is the title of the novel, *The Sun Also Rises*; an anti-war song where the lyric goes "There is a time for everything"; and the epigram of a movie about the Vietnam War that reads "Rejoice O young men in the youth".

Kim I guess they are good examples that prove how Ecclesiastes shook the souls of artists.

Hong The book, *Thus Spoke Zarathustra*, left the same influence on them, but that book was published less than 150 years ago, while Ecclesiastes has been influencing artists for over 3,000 years.

Kim I see. Do you really think money is the answer to everything? What about the many people who were destroyed by money?

Hong Of course, money has astonishing powers of destruction, because a money issue can destroy the relationship between parents and children, siblings, friends, and husband and wife instantly. But after a certain point, money can be directly connected to power.

Kim Since you mentioned it, it reminds me of a dialogue in a movie, titled 'Chinatown'. In the movie, a detective asks a wealthy man in essence, "Why are you so obsessive about money? You don't eat five meals a day instead of three when you have more money." And the rich man says, "It's for the future. The Future!" with 'future' meaning 'power'.

Hong Wouldn't you say that's how rich Jewish people feel about money? Because the only way to avoid being oppressed in the future like they have been for almost 2,000 years is to grab power.

THE STRUGGLE BETWEEN NATIONALISM AND GLOBALISM

Kim You mean rich Jewish people are obsessed with money because ultimately, the only way they can avoid repeating the same sad history is when they have power. However, isn't it possible that they might have the urge to avenge past oppression as well?

Hong Of course, they have. I am sure the urge for revenge has grown greater than ever since 1993.

Kim What happened in 1993?

Hong It was in 1993 that the Jewish film director, Steven Spielberg, directed the movie Schindler's List, which was about the horrible reality of the

Jews in Kraków, Poland, during World War II. The film was the recipient of seven Academy Awards including Best Picture. The movie touched the hearts of people around the world and was acclaimed by many critics as one of the best movies ever made.

Kim I remember watching the movie and being deeply touched by it, but I never connected it with the Jewish people's vengeance. I think it calls for some explanation of the movie.

Hong I would say that the movie really starts with the scene of a little blond girl in a red coat walking down a street in the ghetto and ends with the scene of the body of the same girl being carried to an incinerator on a cart. The prior scenes and the following scenes of the movie are simply over-decorated photo frames of over 2 hour duration. This scheme unequivocally proves the unparalleled genius of Spielberg.

Kim Wouldn't you say that Mr. Schindler's humanity should be also included in the film's theme as the film's title 'Schindler's List' connotes?

Hong Schindler's role was just to give the audience two different viewpoints on the young girl in the red coat. One as a girl walking down the street, and the other as a body being carried to an incinerator.

Kim The red coat the girl was wearing is still vivid in my memory because it was the only tone of color in the mostly black and white movie.

Hong If the girl's coat still remains in your memory, it would have been seared in the memories of Jews. And it will also be firmly tied with the word "vengeance".

Kim Let me summarize the vengeance associated with a movie as follows. First, this film has brought out the remorse in the conscience of people around the world by laying bare the cruelty of human beings, but at the same time, it played a role in rekindling the vengeance of the Jews, which had been suppressed to some extent by the social success of the Jews. Second, anyone who has watched the scene of the atrocities committed against the Jews, as seen in the middle part of the movie covering ghetto scenes for close to 70 minutes, would have been shocked by the non-resistance and helplessness of the Jewish people and the brutality of the Germans.

Thirdly, for this reason, at the end of the 20th century, nearly half a century after the end of World War II, a movie created by a genius rekindled the vengeance of the Jews, which had remained almost dormant as the result of the passage of time and the economic success achieved by Jews.

Hong I think it's a good summary. If I may add one more, the movie was released in 1993, which was about two years after the fall of the former Soviet Union.

Kim Why is that significant?

Hong It is significant because it happened when the capitalists' confidence was at its highest level while the power of the working class reached the lowest level. That's the reason capitalists could exercise their power.

Kim How did the Jewish people's vengeance progress

after the movie?

Hong There is a verse in the Jewish scripture *Talmud* that reads, "Great revenge is to live well." A half century after the end of the war, the Jewish people were living well and they could have convinced themselves that they avenged the cruel persecutions committed against them during the war by 'living well'.

Kim It would have been nice if their vengeance ended there.

Hong There was a good chance that it would have become the case. Moreover, there is a verse in the book of Deuteronomy of the Old Testament that was quoted as an epigram of *Anna Karenina* by Tolstoy: "Vengeance is mine… (and recompense, for the time when their foot shall slip) (Deuteronomy 32:35)." What it means is that you should entrust vengeance to God instead of trying to revenge yourself.

Kim That's right. In fact, the Jews who belong to the top leadership positions in society were satisfied at the success they had achieved in various fields, including the economic field in particular. However, you were saying that the little blond girl in a red coat who appeared in Schindler's List had rekindled a flame in the souls of the Jews, did I get it right?

Hong I think so. I have no intention to argue if anybody criticizes it as being the misguided imagination of a writer like myself. By the way.... What was the other avenue of vengeance in the minds of the rich Jews other than "living well"?

Kim It was to take political power into their hands.

Hong Would it be possible, particularly in a country like the United States? Especially when you consider the Jewish population in the United States is only 5.4 million?

Kim I would say they were pretty confident that it was possible as long as they had enough wealth to influence the outcome of the elections of government officials and to control the mass media. It was from that point on that they pushed forward with globalism as a measure to build massive wealth.

Hong That is an opinion that makes sense. As I just said, the year 1993 was two years after the fall of the former Soviet Union that had been the leader in the communist bloc of the world, which means they were completely free from the ideological threat of communism. They could have thought it was the perfect chance for revenge since it was a time when the income inequality would not incite the rebellion of the working class people. So, they went ahead aggressively with globalism. I wonder what the objective of globalism was.

Kim One major objective is free movement of capital, goods and services across borders. By benefiting all nations, it was supposed to be a win-win game for everybody.

Hong Did globalism succeed?

Kim It failed. In fact, it failed miserably. On the global level, the disparity of wealth between nations and between individuals of each nation increased, compared with pre-globalized era. There are a few exceptional countries.

Hong Who are they?

Kim China and India are major beneficiaries of globalism and their neighboring countries are minor beneficiaries of globalism. Korea as a neighboring country of China is one of rare beneficiary countries. As for individuals, the Wall Street capitalists were major beneficiaries.

Hong Then, who were the main victims of globalism?

Kim American workers who lost their manufacturing jobs; the people of the countries that were devastated by the Asian financial crisis; and the US middle class people who lost their houses and jobs in the wake of the US financial crisis. Come to think of it, the American people were the biggest victims.

Hong If that is the case, then the attempt of the rich people to grasp political power should have ended up a failure, because it would have been impossible to win the support of the American people who had been victimized. Even if they have a full control over the mass media and political funds, they would not have succeeded.

Kim Their failure is attested by Trump's election

victory of 2016. Trump campaigned against globalism, while advocating nationalism. But the final outcome is yet to be known, because their commitment to globalism remains strong and the trend of globalism itself is not easily reversible.

Hong It seems like Trump is upholding nationalism against globalism domestically and he is also upholding the market economy against the non-market economy of China internationally. Do you think Trump will be victorious on both fronts?

Kim He will win on the second front against China's non-market economy. But the result of the first front on globalism is unpredictable. Globalists will not accept their defeat easily. Maybe some kind of compromise is in order.

THE JEWS TAKE THE LEAP FROM THE OPPRESSED TO THE DOMINATOR

Kim Let me change the subject here and ask you a question about the relationship between Trump and Jews. When Trump decided to move U.S. embassy to Jerusalem, didn't it signify an enforcement of Trump's pro-Jews policy?

Hong In 2018, despite strong protest by the Muslim countries of the Middle East, Trump decided to move the US embassy to Jerusalem, which the Israeli government welcomed ardently. However, it may not be altogether a show of Trump's pro-Israel policy.

Kim Then, what was it?

Hong Zionism refers to the traditional Jewish aspiration for the nation-building of a Jewish state in Palestine, which is their homeland, but there is also another movement called Christian Zionism, which is a Christian aspiration to return to the Holy Land.

Kim Is it because the hill of Golgotha is in Jerusalem, and Jesus was crucified there before his resurrection?

Hong That's correct. It was also the birthplace of Jesus. Jerusalem is a commonly shared holy land for the followers of Judaism, Christianity, and Islam. Because of their shared ancestor Abraham, these three religions are collectively called Abrahamism. Theoretically they have no reason to fight each other, but history is stained by bloodshed of these three religions.

Kim When did the conflict between Judaism and Christianity begin?

Hong The Jews had been constantly invaded by neighboring super powers since the 10th century BC, some good examples of which include the invasions by Egypt, Babylon and the Roman Empire. The rebellion of the Jews against the rule of the Roman Empire in the late 2nd century was particularly awesome to the extent that one third of all Roman Empire's Army had to be mobilized by Emperor Hadrianus to suppress the rebellion. During this confrontation, more than 100,000 Jewish people were slaughtered, and the Jewish people had to leave their homeland until the state of Israel was established after World War II.

Kim That rebellion attests to the strong resistance spirit of the Jewish people. I have another question. Why didn't the Romans allow the Jews to return to their homeland, Palestine, after Emperor Constantine The Great adopted Christianity as state religion in the 4th century?

Hong After the adoption of Christianity as the state religion, the suppression of Jews grew worse. And this tradition of suppression continued until the Middle Ages when most Christian countries in Europe persecuted Jewish people by either restricting Jewish settlements and occupations or expelling Jewish people from their countries.

Kim Jews' Zionism succeeded to say the least, because they established the Jewish state of Israel. Why is Jerusalem so important to Jewish people?

Hong To explain that, I think I need to add extra explanations to the three religions. As I told you, Judaism, Christianity, and Islam are the three religions of monotheism that believe in one God: Jehovah, Father and his Son Jesus, Allah. These three religions are collectively called Abrahamism, or "Abrahamic Religion" because of their common ancestor Abraham. The followers of Judaism consider Jerusalem as their most sacred site because the city was built by their ancestor David and his son Solomon. Christians consider Jerusalem as a sacred city as well, because it is where Jesus was born, crucified, and resurrected. And since Jerusalem is the place where the Prophet Mohammed, the founder of Islam, ascended to heavens, Muslims regard it as their third holiest site after Mecca and Medina. That's the reason Jerusalem's histories are stained by bloodsheds of three religious followers. One good example is the war between the Crusades and Muslim powers over the Holy Land that took place in the 12th to 13th centuries.

Kim Now I see that Trump's decision to move the US embassy from Tehran to Jerusalem in 2018 in recognition of the Israeli government's long wish was also for Christian's wish as well.

Hong As mentioned earlier, Jerusalem is a special place for Christianity as well as for Evangelical Christians because it is where Jesus was resurrected. It is correct to say that when Trump moved the US embassy to the city, he made the decision as a devout Protestant believer.

Kim Is it also called Zionism by Christians?

Hong The desire of Jews to return to Jerusalem is called Zionism, but in Christianity, and in Protestantism in particular, the wish for the return to the Holy Land is called Christian Zionism. Despite this identical spirit of Zionism of two religions, the animosity Jews and Romans developed against each other when the Jews rebelled against the

Romans towards the end of the 2nd century AD, and when Jews later refused to convert to Christianity under the Roman Empire changed into religious hostility of Romans against Jews. This hostility then spread into Christian nations that became part of the Roman Empire causing series of persecutions of Jews by European Christian nations, culminated with the Auschwitz Holocaust.

Kim Isn't there a basis to say that the hostility between two religions is due to the differences in their religious doctrines?

Hong Well. I do not know much about it myself. But the Jews showed a tendency to look down on Christians' belief of the Trinity, claiming Jesus as the son of God.

Kim Isn't it possible that Jews look down on Christians out of pride for using Jewish sacred scripture as the Old Testament section of the Bible?

Hong It could be one reason.

Kim I remember Pope John Paul, who is from Poland, had discreetly expressed regrets for the three wrongdoings Christianity did in the past. What were those three mistakes, I don't remember....

Hong As far as I remember, the first was the Crusaders' atrocities committed in the 12th and 13th centuries, the second was about the religious trials during the Middle Ages, and the third was the fault of the Vatican which kept silent about the Jewish massacre. At any rate, the apology of Pope Paul was a demonstration of the great courage of Christianity.

Kim The Nazi's Auschwitz Holocaust was the most horrible of all Jewish persecutions, which had continued for 2,500 years.

Hong Yes. In the future, no ethnic entity will be subjected to such barbaric persecution because the eyes and ears of the world are now linked through social media. Besides, the United States that emerged as the world's super power through the first and the second world wars became the second Jewish nation after Israel, where Jewish people elevated themselves from a persecuted group to a dominating group.

Kim When you think about how well the Jews are doing in practically every field in America, except for the brick-and-mortar type manufacturing field, particularly in finance, journalism, arts, cinema, academics and law, wouldn't you say it's almost a miracle?

Hong It is truly a wondrous miracle, made by a single ethnic group. You have to admit that the Jewish people who overcame so many adversities with an invincible spirit were different from other ethnic groups at their very roots.

Kim Can you think of any statistics that specifically attest to the superiority of the Jews?

Hong I wrote them down on my smart phone. Let me check. The Jews account for 50 percent of America's highest-level intellectuals; 40 percent of the Nobel Prize winners in the science and economics areas; 20 percent of professors at America's most prestigious colleges; 40% of the partners in law firms in New York and Washington; and 60 percent of script writers, directors and producers of the 50 highest gross-earning movies.... The list goes on and on.

Kim Just give me one more, because it's really intimidating.

Hong All right. Let me give you one more. The Jews accounted for 50 percent of the World's Chess Champions.

Kim I have to admit the Jews are a superior ethnic group, but I wonder how they are rated in their contribution to society.

Hong Do you remember the marches of the black people held in 1965 from Selma, Alabama, to Montgomery in an effort to register black voters in the South?

Kim I can clearly remember watching them on the news, because I was married in 1965 and the marches happened while I was on my honeymoon

Hong Then you will remember quite a few young white people marching along in the crowd of mostly blacks. Most of these white people are Jewish. It is something only the descendants of people who had been severely persecuted in the past would do. Then came Rev. King's speech, "I have a dream....", that echoed through Washington, and several decades later, America saw the election of a black president whose slogan was "change."

Kim I remember those young white people, but I simply thought they were some conscientious and brave white young people.

Hong That is not all. In America, it is clearly written in their legal codes that torturing a suspect is illegal even if the suspect is accused of terrorist activities, and that law is enforced strictly. That's the reason the CIA had to lock up terrorists in Guantanamo, Cuba. This is possible in America because the Jews are the dominant majority in important legal positions. It is a good example of the Exceptionalism that made America the world's leader by swearing by principle instead of power.

Kim It seems that America has sort of a sacred power that no other super powers of the past possessed, and I think that power comes from believing in the idea of equality and the commitment of helping the weak and resisting the powerful.

But I've never thought that it was because of the influence of the Jewish people. By the way, is that spirit of "helping the weak, resisting the powerful" still valid in America?

THE ESSENCE OF THE AMERICAN PRESS, AMERICAN EXCEPTIONALISM

Hong It is the American press that has been carrying on the tradition of the very idea, which is American Exceptionalism, and at the center of that American press is the Jewish people.

Kim Can you give me some specific examples?

Hong The New York Times and the Washington Post made America end the Vietnam War sooner than later by elevating the status of Ho Chi Minh of Vietnam to the same level as George Washington of the United States. And a linguist from MIT dubbed by the New York Times as the "American Conscience" was banned from entering Israel for having branded the Israeli leader as a terrorist against Palestine. These two newspapers were founded by Jewish families who have been running them until recently, and the linguist from MIT was a Jew to the bone. These are examples of American Exceptionalism.

Kim How do you assess the influence the Jewish people left on American pop culture? I am asking because it seems there are people who have negative views about it.

Hong Do you happen to remember the half-time performance of the 50th American Super Bowl game?

Kim I remember watching Beyoncé performing at an American football stadium on TV. She showed some amazing dance moves. It made me feel spontaneously exhilarated.

Hong It is natural for you to become exhilarated, because you cannot fail to feel the passion.

Kim What do you mean by passion?

Hong I mean the passion that you need to stand with the weak and resist the powerful. Beyoncé let her blond hair flow loose, but all the female dancers were wearing berets, which was intended to recall the image of Che Guevara, the legendary rebel and the hero of the Cuban revolution even though some assert it symbolizes 'Black Panther'.

Kim I never noticed it. Come to think of it, I remember reading a news article about the half-time show of the 50th Super Bowl game having too many political overtones.

Hong In addition, if you look at the performance from a bird's-eye view, the dancers were creating an X-shaped formation. That was pointing to a legendary black rebel named Malcom X. There is an interesting story about the reason that rebel picked X for his last name. It is said that he picked it to obscure his last name because black women have been nothing but sex toys for white men. Such creative ideas were possible because it was a performance designed by Jews. If an ordinary white man had designed the performance, it would have been a cliché performance by a star with flowing blond hair.

Kim What does political resistance have to do with creativity?

Hong Whatever form a resistance takes, it all starts with the idea of equality. If you look at it, the Internet also came from the same idea. You just told me that Beyoncé's performance was exhilarating. It was exhilarating because it had the idea of equality and the spirit of resistance at its foundation. That's what passion is all about.

Kim Is it true that Psy was able to earn a global-scale reputation within such a short time because of help from Jews? Then, does it also have anything to do with the Jews' idea of equality and the spirit of resistance?

Hong Sure it does. His Gangnam Style is about mockingly describing the petty bourgeois, which is the typical Korean nouveau riche who enjoys showing off their wealth, enjoying riding horses, but has no brains. There was a young Jewish man who believed that the song that mocked the rich people of the world through the Korean nouveau riche had both significance and potential for commercial success. When Gangnam Style hit record hit number on YouTube, he called Psy from America, and made Psy an offer Psy couldn't refuse. It was to use the Korean lyrics without a change of a word. Wasn't he being true to a Jew?

Kim In what way, do you mean?

Hong He would never have been able to make such a suggestion unless he had the blood of Jews who had to be scattered throughout the world for generations. In fact, all human languages are supposed to sound similar to aliens, because the images behind languages are the same. Besides, that young agent had enough experience with sacred Jewish scriptures whose meanings can be conveyed correctly only when they are recited in Hebrew, even though you don't know the exact meaning of the words.

Kim Then, was Psy's global reputation credited to the help from that young agent?

Hong It was more like helping each other, than getting

help. But the Jews' idea of racial equality played a critical role. In fact, Psy's path to stardom was rather simple. He had Psy invited to an American talk show and teach a singer named Britney Spears "horse dance steps", and he also made him dance with Madonna who had a concert in New York City at the time. Everybody knows the rest of the story.

Kim The connection between Jews and the popular arts is amazing. The world in which we live in now is the world where any talented young man can be catapulted into global fame, isn't it?

Hong That is not true. If there was a man who was Asian like Psy but of Japanese nationality, he would never have been picked up by the agent. The same logic applies to BTS, a boy group that is sensationally popular lately, as it applies to Psy.

Kim What is the reason?

Hong The epitome of Jewish persecution is the Holocaust. Japan was one of the "axis partners" of Germany along with Italy.

Kim Do you mean the Jews' sentiments are so persistent to be involved even in that area?

Hong Sure. If you look at the foreign-made cars Israel imported in 2017, Hyundai and Kia automobiles outpaced Toyota by ranking number one and two, and Benz did not even make it to the top ten list.

Kim That is truly amazing.

Hong That's not all. Google at the initial stage of smart phone development would never have allowed the access of the source code of Android OS so generously, had its partner been Sony, not Samsung. It means Samsung's current position as world's top mobile phone seller has a lot to do with the country Samsung belongs to.

Kim It was very fortunate that Korea could become friendly with Jews due to a certain course of past world history.

Hong It's not just a coincidence of history. Koreans and Korean religions have tendencies that resonate with Jews and Judaism. It is the opposite with the case of Islam and Christian countries in the West.

Kim Why is that?

Hong If I may start with tendency, Koreans share many similarities with Jews. Both Korean and Jewish peoples have constantly suffered because of surrounding super powers throughout history. They also share the same commitment to educating their children, so much so that their children are among the top students at prestigious colleges in the US. In terms of religion, Christians in Korea respect Jews as being the same race as Jesus Christ, unlike Christians in Western countries who consider Jews as the people who killed Jesus. Perhaps it has a lot to do with the fact that Korea is the only country in the world where Confucianism, founded upon the idea of worshiping ancestors, remains in its original form. For these reasons, the two peoples will continue to remain friendly, as we have seen in the case of Psy, which is a good example of cooperation between two peoples. The truth is, when considered from the perspective of Jews, there are not many peoples in the world they can maintain true friendship with.

Kim Why is that?

Hong It is difficult for the Jews to become true friends with Christian countries, particularly the Christian countries in the West, because of their history of having suffered and been persecuted by them. And with Islamic countries, there are obstacles associated with territorial and religious disputes. It is difficult with Japan, too, because, as I've mentioned earlier, Japan was one of the "Axis Partners" of Germany during World War II. In the end, it leaves only a few countries, such as China, India and Korea. But with China, it is a country that might become a supposititious enemy of America, which can be considered as the second home to the global Jewish population, and that might work unfavorably. India doesn't seem to have any negative element and India's advanced math skills might be attractive to Jews. However, in terms of ethnic background, the majority of the high-class in India's caste system are Aryans. It will not be easy for Jews to forget the fact that the German Nazis persecuted

Jews under the racist doctrine known as "Aryan Supremacy".

Kim I'm sure the Jewish influence will continue to grow in all areas, because their wealth will increase exponentially thanks to the combination of their intelligence and a well-established Jewish society. How far will their influence extend? Is it possible that they will turn the world into a caste society where they occupy the world's ruling class consisting of only a small number of people?

Hong Money may be "the answer to everything", but it also has astonishingly destructive power. One example is the case of their unreasonable push to give the Nobel Prize in literature a few years ago to a Jewish songwriter in his late 70s who was popular in the 1960s. This is the kind of action that could make those from global literary circles into their enemies instantly. If they continue to resort to such extremely arrogant behavior, one will never know if the truth about "history repeating itself" will come to reality again. That is a proverb that Jews have to keep deep in their hearts.

Part III

TRADE WAR BETWEEN THE UNITED STATES AND CHINA: WHAT IS KOREA'S CHOICE IN THE WAR?

PROLOGUE

After having long conversations with Professor Kim, I went to the National Library for almost two weeks and spent most of the day there. I wanted to make notes on the conversations I had with him because I might be able to use them in my next novel, and I also wanted to research more about the parts of the conversations that I was not familiar with. Besides, I liked the relaxing atmosphere of the library, and the fact that the lunch I could get at the library cafeteria was superior to what I could get in restaurants but cost only four dollars also worked as a big contributing factor.

But towards the end of the two weeks when I finished

making notes of the conversations with Prof. Kim and reviewed them, I realized they had more potential than as my personal notes, because significant parts of the conversations were addressing common knowledge that today's young people would need to live in a society. I wanted to turn it into a book, if only a small booklet, and wanted to share our conversations with the young generation who will be the main players in our near future.

So, I decided to look for another scholar whose academic specialty is different from economics professor Kim so that I can have conversations on a broader range of topics and expand our discussion.

That's how I came upon Professor Lee, who is the same age as me and studied economics and sociology with particular insights into China. Parts III and IV of this book are the record of conversations I had with Professor Lee.

Professor Lee is currently teaching the process of Korea's economic growth at a national university in Mongolia for one semester a year. He is one of the very rare scholars who don't have a positive view on the outlook of the Chinese economy and he also has a rather critical view of the North Korean leadership.

GLOBAL LEADERSHIP: DOES IT BELONG TO THE UNITED STATES OR CHINA?

Hong History is truly unpredictable. After World War II, the world came to face the Cold War, and for the next 45 years, the world turned under the so-called Bi-polar System in which the US and the Soviet Union were the commanders of the capitalist bloc and the communist bloc of the world, respectively. Then the world's order of hegemony was restructured into the so-called Uni-polar system with the United States rising above to the top in the wake of the collapse of the former Soviet Union in 1991. How long do you think this uni-polar system will last?

Lee Well... China overtook Japan in 2010 and emerged as the second largest economy in the world and posed a challenge around mid-2010s to the American hegemony. It all happened just about a quarter century after the collapse of the former Soviet Union.

Hong In what form did China pose a challenge?

Lee China did not hide its intention to compete with the United States over world hegemony by announcing policies such as "One Belt One Road" in 2013 and "Made in China 2025" in 2015.

Hong Does China actually have enough power to compete with the United States for hegemony? Or is it their ill-informed attempt resulting from poor advice from experts, like the former Soviet Union did against the United States in the past? As you may be aware, numerous scholars defined the former Soviet Union as a "rising power" and the United States as the "declining power" as recently as in the early 1980s.

Lee In fact, until the fall of the Berlin Wall at the end of 1989, the so-called “historicism”, a term used by Karl Marx, had been popular in academic towers.

Hong What does that word signify?

Lee In short, it was about communization of the world as the inevitability of history. A British scholar named Carl Popper refuted this idea in his book, *The Poverty of Historicism.*

Hong What was the main argument of that book?

Lee It was called “piecemeal social engineering”. Just as an engineer would fix a broken machine and make it even better, a society needs to fix its problems by freely discussing and criticizing them and gradually improving to become a better society.

Hong It just struck me that the logic might be applied to parenting. Parents cannot determine the future of their children, and all they can do is to watch over them and influence them little by little while they are growing.... At any rate, does China have enough power to compete with the United States in the hegemony war?

Lee I cannot tell if it has enough power, but I am sure China will at least mount a challenge to the United States. And the previously mentioned "One Belt One Road" and "Made in China 2025" policies are that very challenge.

Hong Wouldn't it be meaningful at this stage for us to try to evaluate the qualifications of China and the United States to verify which one is more eligible as a world leader?

Lee There wouldn't be much dispute about the United States coming out on top.

Hong Why does the world acknowledge the leadership of the United States in general?

Lee I can identify three reasons. First, America is a land of immigrants where 55 percent of its population is white, 40 percent is African-Americans and Hispanics, and 5 percent, Asians and others. And the majority of the white immigrants are descendants of people who had been oppressed politically, economically, or religiously in their homelands. For that reason, Americans tend to sympathize with marginalized people and resist people in power more than others.

Hong Apparently that background laid the ground for "a classless middle-class society" of America, a similar example of which we cannot find in history.

Lee That's right. Such belief in equality is the second reason America should be the leader. America is said to be a society that is more open than any other democratic societies that have ever existed, and such an open society is not possible without belief in equality. America was able to triumph over the former Soviet Union precisely because it was an open society built on the belief in equality.

Hong So, that's how America became the birthplace of such companies like Google in the early 21st century.

Lee Do you know what Google's motto is?

Hong No, I don't. What is it?

Lee It is the "universal access of information." The idea behind the motto is that, be it the president of a country or an ordinary college student, they are all entitled to share the same information. That is what truly changed the world forever.

Hong If I may exaggerate a little bit, one can say that this motto is cemented in people's mind as the Bill of Rights for people around the world. So what is the third reason?

Lee Nowadays, there is criticism that the American press is too commercialized, biased and sometimes provocative, but still, you can say that it is the fairest and the most righteous press on the planet. Its fairness has been tarnished after business people became their owners, but originally, the owners of the American press were mostly Jews, and they had the courage to resist power regardless of ethnic, national, religious and ideological differences because they suffered throughout history more than any other ethnic groups. Some of the good examples are the anti-Vietnam War editorials of the New York Times and Washington Post in the 1960s.

Hong I have no intention of trying to refute your claims, but I have to admit it is pretty sad that the next generation journalists of such wonderful newspapers are now walking on eggshells around the businessmen owners. Let's change the subject now and would you explain why China is not fit to be a global leader?

Lee I will give you three reasons. First, if China becomes the global leader, China is likely to become excessively self-assertive and egoistic because per capita income of its people is too low. The population of China is 1.4 billion, which is about one fifth of the world population. Among them, 92 percent are the Han Chinese, and the other 8 percent consists of 50 plus minor ethnic groups. If China becomes the global leader, the poor Han Chinese that accounts for one fifth of the world population will reign over the rest four fifths of the global population. This ratio will be too troubling for global citizens to accept China as the leader.

Hong Is America less troubling to the global community?

Lee On the other hand, the population of America is

about 350 million, which is much less than that of China. Even though the American population consists of various ethnic groups, the number of whites is just about half the entire population. That is a big difference from China where the Han Chinese population is overwhelming.

Hong What is the second reason?

Lee China is run by one despotic political party, and that is the critical weakness for China to be considered qualified as a global leader. Leaders in China are not elected through referendums. People of one nation with even the slightest amount of consciousness would find the indirect election by one despotic political party unacceptable. Given that, imagine how the global community will view it.

Hong That is a very convincing argument.

Lee The third reason China is not qualified to be a global leader is the hidden vengeance that Chinese people have deep in their hearts. It is a common sense that leaders should not hold any vengeance against those they lead.

Hong What exactly is that "hidden vengeance"?

Lee The vengeance originates from the so-called "100 years of humiliation." China suffered cruel humiliations from Western super powers and Japan for exactly 107 years until Mao Zedong established the People's Republic of China, and it covers the period from the first Opium War that broke out in 1842 to the second Opium War, the 1931 Mukden Incident, and the 1938 Nanjing massacre.

Hong But "hidden vengeance" is not something they cannot forget forever, is it? Even though there is no guarantee that it will disappear only with the passage of time.

Lee The problem is human nature. It is human nature that when you become stronger, you tend to rekindle your thirst for revenge. Even if it doesn't necessarily mean direct revenge, it can be at least used to justify unequal relationships.

Hong When do you think the world will be ready to accept Chinese leadership?

Lee I think it will take the Chinese time to experience

economic prosperity and political freedom and tolerance for at least two generations, or about 50 years. If China experiences and gets used to prosperity and tolerance as a global economic super power for 50 years, then, China will be qualified to become a global leader.

Hong You mean, the United States will keep the status of being the global leader for at least half a century from now. If that's true, the Korea-US relations seem more important than I'd thought.

SPECIAL RELATIONS BETWEEN KOREA AND THE UNITED STATES

Hong Wouldn't you say that the relationship between Korea and the US has been historically very unique compared with relationships of other two countries? I am sure there are a number of characteristics to their relationship, but can you list a few important ones?

Lee I can identify five characteristics of the Korea-US relationship. I can easily answer your question because I am addressing similar subjects in my lectures at the college in Mongolia.

Hong That's great. Perhaps you can treat me as one of your students in your lecture at the college in Mongolia. I will just listen to you without interruption until your lecture is over.

Lee All right, but you can interrupt me any time. Let me give you five titles first: lack of hostility, historic relations, religious relations, economic relations, and military relations. First, let me start with the lack of hostility. As you know, Korea was liberated from Japan after having been under its colonial rule for 36 years when Japan made unconditional surrender to the United States. Unlike other countries on the Pacific coast, Korea is one of the few countries that have never been in colonial or hostile relations with America, or any other Western country for that matter. When you experience colonial rule, the ruled parties are destined to grudge hostility against the ruling to a certain degree.

If the ruling country is an advanced Western country, even though most of the ruling countries were advanced Western countries except for Japan, it will be considered just as a "Western ruler" from the perspective of the ruled people, no matter what specific Western country it is. For that reason, countries like Indonesia that were colonized by the Netherlands, or India that was colonized by England, might hold hostile feelings against the US because it's the same Western country. But Korea was never colonized by any Western country. Korea was only colonized or humiliated by neighbors: Japan and China.

Second, let's look at the historical relationship. Korea's neighboring super powers such as Japan, Russia, and China had been in a confrontational relationship with the United States at one point. Japan was the enemy of the United States during World War II, Russia was in an intensely confrontational relationship with the United States as the leader of the Communist bloc during the Cold War era, and China clashed with the United States on the Korean peninsula during the Korean War in the early 1950s. As of today, Japan is an ally of the United States. But whatever the reason, the fact that the US dropped atomic bombs on Japan at the end of World War

II is not something that can easily be erased from Japanese memories.

Korea, on the other hand, was liberated from Japan with the help of the United States. Korea was one of the poorest countries in the world at the time of liberation, but as of 2018, Korea has grown to become the 11th largest economy in the world in terms of GDP. This remarkable growth was supported by friendly relations with the United States. In this regard, Koreans have a sense of gratitude and an affinity for the United States.

Third, let's look at the religious relationship. The difference between humans and animals is that humans have languages and religions. And human religions dominate most of human activities. There are many religions, such as Confucianism, Buddhism, Christianity, Islam, Hinduism and Judaism, but of all these religions, Koreans accepted Confucianism, Buddhism, and Christianity as the main religions. There are 13.7 million Christians (9.6 million Protestants, 3.9

million Catholics, 0.2 million for minor denomination) and 7.6 million Buddhists out of the 50 plus million Korean population. It makes Korea the only country in the world with a relatively good balance of three major religions, Confucianism, Christianity and Buddhism.

What is unique about religions in Korea is that each of these three religions has a different place of worship: Confucianism-based ancestral rituals at home; Buddhist-based Zen meditations at Buddhist temples; and Christian liturgies mostly in urban churches. Korean Christians are unmatched in terms of their religious enthusiasm by any others, as we can see how committed they are in their early morning prayer and overseas evangelism. Perhaps, the main reason is that, for Koreans who were never colonized by the Western countries, Christianity might have greatly appealed as a rational Western religion.

The English author of *Utopia* said that the fear of God is a fundamental force that maintains a Utopia. Another Russian author stressed the necessity of Christianity by saying, "If there is no God, anything is possible for a man in a negative sense." The United States is a devout Christian nation, so much so that they abide by the tradition of using the Bible for the President's swearing-in ceremony and for a witness testimony in court. Lately there have been some signs that Christian influence has been declining in American society, but it is bouncing back as we see how the US President Trump starts a cabinet meeting with a prayer.

You can say that the relationship between Korea and the United States is more than just an ally, because their bonding is founded upon the fact that both countries have strong Christian tradition, and that clearly distinguishes Korea's relationship with the United States from any other Eastern Asian countries'.

Fourth, let's talk about economic relations. Korea's economy is heavily dependent on exports, which account for almost half of the national GDP. Korea being a country with scarce natural resources and without particularly outstanding tourism resources, exports of manufactured goods are more important than in any other neighboring countries. The United States has been the major market for Korea, and that played a critical role in the economic growth of Korea. As of 2017, China is the biggest importer of Korean goods followed by the United States, with both countries accounting for 26 percent and 23 percent of Korean exports, respectively. However, the fact that China is the biggest importer of Korean goods loses much of its significance in view of a fact that majority of their imports are half-finished goods such as semi-conductor, petroleum-derivatives, and chemical products, and the final destination of those half-finished Korean products are mostly the U.S. other than China.

With regard to the service industry, there is something that distinguishes Korea-US relationships from the US relationships with Korea's neighbors: Korea is fairly open to the US service industry, particularly to the US movie industry that is clearly ahead of the Korean movie industry. The Korean fandom of American movies, in particular, is undeniably far above that of other countries.

The pop entertainment area is the same. The Korean boy group BTS ranked number one on the Billboard chart in America even though the group sang most of their songs in Korean. The success of BTS in America proves that the bond between Korea and the United States in pop entertainment and arts areas is so mutually benefiting that they seem to share the same DNA. There is a clear difference with regard to other countries in this matter.

Fifth, let's look at the military relations. In 1950, Korea became the battlefield of a proxy war between the Western camp and the Communist camp while America and the former Soviet Union were in a confrontational relation under the Cold War system. The Communist camp consisted of the North Korean and Chinese troops, while the

Western camp by the US and the South Korean troops. The three-year war resulted in 50,000 US casualties.

Then, in the mid-1960s, the United States fell prey to the false logic of their military-industrial complex that claimed, "Vietnam First, US Westcoast Next" and decided to deploy US troops to the Vietnam War. This war, however, did not end as easily as they'd expected. When America was struggling in the war as numerous young Americans joined anti-war campaigns, crying out "Ho Chi Minh is the same as Washington in the US", the Korean government deployed over 5,000 Korean soldiers to join the US troops, willingly taking the risk of their sacrifices. Of course, the deployment of Korean soldiers brought to Korea economic benefits from the US in return, but the deployment would not have been possible had there not been a long history of military alliance between Korea and the United States.

Then towards the end of the 1970s, President Carter planned to withdraw US forces stationed in Korea, but it did not materialize. Later on, the Korean government took the initiative to bring all US military bases in Korea to Pyeongtaek in 2018. It is the single largest US military base in the world, built on a site as big as the central region of the US capital, Washington DC. It is a small city in itself that can accommodate up to 80,000 people, capable of serving US Army, Navy and Air Force because of its proximity to Pyeongtaek Port where the nuclear submarine can be stationed and Gunsan Air Force Base that is equipped with large-scale runways. It is also not far from a site where THAAD is deployed.

Currently, Korea is paying half the cost of having the US forces stationed in Korea, but it costs the US government far less to have its military forces stationed in Korea than in its mainland. All these facts work in favor to keep the military alliance between Korea and the US strong for a long time, and to make it a win-win game for both Korea and the US. From the perspective of Korea, the military alliance can ensure regional stability that is necessary for economic development, and from the perspective of the US, they can have a military presence in the Pacific region at a low cost.

I should stop here because I might bore you if I continue.

Hong Thanks for the explanation. I learned a lot. Surely, it is a great pleasure to listen to a good lecture. But there is something I must ask you. Do you think there is a possibility for the US to withdraw their forces from its Pyeongtaek base within the next ten years?

Lee The possibility is very thin. It took the US 70 years to secure its military grounding in East Asia after World War II. It is rapidly gaining strategic importance because of China's emergence. The US might make contradictory diplomatic gestures depending on circumstances, but it will not be easy for them to give up the 70 years of hard work and sacrifices that easily, particularly after the rise of China as a competing military power of the world.

Hong I take it as to say that the US will not withdraw its military forces voluntarily, unless the Korean people rise in protest and demand the closing of the Pyeongtaek base.

Lee I think so. For the sake of its national interest, the US is not to take Korea lightly. And the US military facilities in Pyeongtaek base will continue to be upgraded with the latest technologies and before long, it will undoubtedly become the symbol of superior US military-related technologies. Korea surely will be the beneficiary of their technological power as well, because all technological innovations in the military sector are destined to flow into the private sector.

Hong There is no doubt the US needs to keep its military base in Pyeongtaek as a measure for a possible confrontation with China. Given that, I think it's time to talk about China now.

CUT-THROAT TRADE WAR BETWEEN THE US AND CHINA

Hong As of late 2018, the United States and China are waging a trade war. Was the war really unavoidable?

Lee In mid-2017, Trump ordered the United States Trade Representative (USTR) to investigate China's violation of the U.S.'s intellectual property rights, while at the same time calling Xi Jinping to notify him of the fact. Xi Jinping should have realized the seriousness of the situation right away.

Hong On what basis did Trump make that order?

Lee The legal basis was Section 301 of the U.S.

Trade Act of 1974. And USTR submitted its investigation reports in March 2018.

Hong So, the US government imposed special tariffs on Chinese products in mid-2018, and China responded by imposing tariffs on US products in a tit-for-tat strategy.

Lee Yes. And that was a serious mistake on the side of China. When the USTR reports were released, China should have appealed to WTO against the unfairness of the US government's decision on tariffs based on these reports, instead of retaliating tit-for-tat. This international legal process would have prevented the US from taking more drastic measures immediately afterwards.

Hong What were the US's drastic measures?

Lee The U.S. created a joint Western front with advanced Western countries such as the United Kingdom, Germany and France in addition to Japan and fought back together against China. Trump's first move was to integrate the resistance of the governments of the advanced Western countries against the Chinese-made high-tech and telecommunication products. He hoped that during the process, the China's non-market economy under the one-party dictatorship would stand out as an apparent strategic competitor of the Western market economy system.

Hong Did Trump succeed in this approach?

Lee He succeeded, indeed. China fell into the deep trap set up by Trump by responding with a tit-for-tat policy against Trump's tariff policy.

Hong Didn't China notice that deep trap?

Lee That's what I cannot understand myself. Trump claimed throughout his election campaign in 2016 that Americans lost their jobs to China and that America had to bring them back. Trump had a firm commitment to rebuilding the American manufacturing industry, so much so that even in his inaugural address, he included the phrase, "The wealth of our middle class has been ripped from their homes and then redistributed across the entire world."

Hong Was there a reason he targeted China in particular?

Lee If you break down the US trade deficit, about 50 percent is due to China, followed by 15 percent to EU and another 15 percent due to Japan and Mexico, and the other 20 percent to countries around the world. So, it is natural that China became its main target. But there is something else. In 2015, China poured fuel on this fiery situation.

Hong What did China do?

Lee In 2015, China dared to declare to the world "Made in China 2025," which was China's national blueprint for the future, but it was more like sort of a manifesto comparable to The *Communist Manifesto*, which could be considered as the Communist Bible written by Karl Marx and Friedrich Engels.

Hong Considering a manifesto is a type of political statement in its nature, I wonder what "Made in China 2025" was about.

Lee In short, it was a statement about their strategy to seize hegemony by state capitalism. There is only one way to prevent the realization of this

21st century version of the *Communist Manifesto*, which can be billed as the *State Capitalism Manifesto*. It is to decouple China, a lone nation of state capitalism, from the markets of advanced Western countries.

Hong You mean tariff was the bait Trump had tossed to China, and the trap Trump had dug was "decoupling China from the markets of the advanced Western countries." How is this 'decoupling' possible?

Lee By cutting off a portion of a globalized China's supply chain, it is quite possible. That is my personal opinion. Of course, I might be wrong. Therefore, I ask you to accept it as just a theory.

Hong I've never thought that China's declaration of "Made in China 2025" had such a significant impact. What part of that declaration motivated advanced Western countries including the United States to unite against China?

Lee It was absolutely no wonder that the Obama administration of the United States as well as the leaderships of the advanced nations such as Japan and Western countries were shocked when China announced its blueprint for the future under the title "Made in China 2025" in 2015. According to this blueprint, the percentage of the Chinese-domestic content of core materials is stipulated to be at least 40 percent by 2020 and 70 percent by 2025 for all products for Chinese domestic market.

Hong Then they simply can choose to stay away from Chinese markets.

Lee It is difficult to survive in the global market if you ignore the Chinese market that serves one fifth of the world population because of the loss of productivity increase from scale of economy. But if China increases the Chinese-domestic content of core materials to 70 percent, technologies on core materials will be naturally transferred to China. Then the Western countries including the US will lose their competitiveness in high tech industries that they have today, and consequently, the future of the Western countries including the US will be gloomy.

Hong China announced that manifesto while Obama was the US president. What measures did the Obama administration take in response?

Lee The Obama administration decided to form a free trade zone with countries including those in the Asian Pacific region that could supply products to replace Chinese-made exports as measures to contain China. That's how the TPP (Trans-Pacific Partnership) came about. It was quite different from what the Trump administration did, which was more aggressive measures of imposing sweeping tariffs on China.

Hong But I understand that the TPP lost its momentum since Trump removed the US from the TPP.

Lee It did. From the beginning, the measures the Obama administration took to respond to "Made in China 2025" were foolish. The idea of decreasing the US dependency on China by forming a free trade zone called TPP with Pacific countries excluding China was nonsense at best. The Obama administration simply didn't realize that China was controlled by a one-party dictatorship, especially by 25 members of the Politburo and further by 9 Politburo members of the all-powerful Politburo Standing Committee. It is estimated that over 60 percent of all major Chinese industries were under the direct control of the Communist Party.

Hong How does the ruling structure of Chinese industries affect the usefulness of the TPP?

Lee None of the TPP member countries can afford to take the risk of possible retaliation by the Chinese communist party if they attempt to replace Chinese exports to the US with their own goods. It is because while the leaders in China have no limits on their terms, leaders of other countries have to maintain the support of their constituents. In this sense, even Japanese leaders may not feel immune to fears of China's retaliation.

Hong Can you give me some specific examples?

Lee Suppose about 10 percent of Chinese population, about 130 million, travel overseas in a year, and suppose the Chinese Communist Party covertly issues travel ban to a certain country, it will have significant impact on the economy of the targeted countries, particularly regions of tourist attractions. This situation may even incite a political instability in the region.

Hong What happened in Korea after the decision was made on the deployment of THAAD on the Korean peninsula should be a good example.

Lee That's right. When it was decided to deploy the US military THAAD on the Korean peninsula, China banned all tourist companies in China from sending Chinese tourists to Korea. As a result, a lot of Koreans who were working in tourism-related service industries lost their jobs, and the infrastructures associated with tourism were left abandoned as unused facilities. What is more surprising is that the Chinese government is still denying they ever took such measures. Besides, it forced the Korean government to make all kinds of appeasing gestures to lift the ban before they finally allowed Chinese tourists to visit Korea little by little, all the while acting pompous as if they were training the Korean government as one would train its dog.

Hong That is such a preposterous policy. Personally, I never had any anti-Chinese feelings before, but after having experienced this incident, I might turn into an anti-Chinese Korean.

Lee I can absolutely relate to how you feel. Fortunately, Korea is not heavily dependent on tourism revenue, but the Chinese measures could have been near fatal to countries whose revenue is heavily dependent on tourism, or countries with a large part of the population working in tourism-related businesses. Therefore, through the case of Korea, China delivered a clear message to countries that depend heavily on tourism revenues about what could happen to them and their administrations if they cross the Chinese government.

Hong Wouldn't China's threat keep growing exponentially over the years? Because the percentage of Chinese who travel overseas may drastically increase from the current 10 percent to let's say, 30 percent which is an average for developed countries, fully realizing the security impact of Chinese policy.

Lee It will. So, the US government ordered the US Department of Defense to submit reports on this issue in March 2017, and the investigative reports, signed by the Secretary of the US Department of Defense were released in July 2018. With these reports, the US government exposed to the entire world how China was arrogantly brandishing its power against weaker countries.

Hong Isn't the scale of China's economy just as threatening to the world as the number of Chinese tourists? As far as I understand, the size of the Chinese economy is threatening just in itself because it is about 70 percent of the size of the US economy, but what seems to be more terrifying is the fact that such a massive economy is under the control and rule of a single Chinese Communist Party.

Lee That is precisely the reason most countries, not to mention globally acknowledged companies, cannot counterattack China out of fear of retaliation. It is comparable to a situation where countries and companies around the world are expecting somebody to step out and hang a bell on the neck of the cat. Ultimately, the US has to step forward and do the deed because the US is ahead of China in terms of scale of economy by 10:7. Then the US will be followed by other developing countries whose manufacturing capacity is good enough to replace Chinse manufacturers.

Hong By doing so, the world will be able to avoid the situation where the state capitalism of China's one-party dictatorship, instead of the communism as the former Soviet Union had once tried, is replacing democratic capitalism. Did I get it right?

Lee That's right. If the United States does not do something aggressive to contain China, China will overtake the United States in terms of the scale of economy. If that happens, many low-income countries around the world, beginning with African countries that prefer prolonged one-party or one-man dictatorships, will prefer the Chinese way of rule, and the influence of the United States will decline significantly.

DYNAMICS OF THE TRILATERAL KOR-US-CHINA RELATIONSHIP AS EXPOSED BY THE THAAD DEPLOYMENT ON THE KOREAN PENINSULA

Hong I am surprised at the reactions of both China and the United States, related with the deployment of THAAD on the Korean peninsula. The first is the reaction of China, which was about putting a ban on Chinese tourists from visiting Korea, and the second is the reaction of the United States that sent a warning to China through its Department of Defense. I want to hear your opinion on this.

Lee First, let me walk you through the process of the reports being released by the US Dept. of Defense. Even though the US Secretary of State is in official hierarchy over the Secretary of

Defense, one aircraft carrier with 6,000 crews has the capacity to carry the entire personnel of the Department of State.

Hong So, the warning signed by the Secretary of Defense against China for having restricted Chinese tourists from visiting Korea had a special significance.

Lee That's right. Besides, I've heard that they took such special caution and consideration in handling the matter that it took over one year to write those reports. Simply put, the US government took China's restriction on traveling to Korea as a low-level attack on its ally. It will not be easy for China to take similar measures against other countries from now on.

Hong I wonder how China came up with the idea of using the restriction of tourists as retaliation against THAAD deployment.

Lee I would say that China emulated the method the US frequently uses. The US economy accounting for a quarter of the entire world economy, the US has often refused to open its market to her adversaries. On the other hand, China's population accounting for one fifth of world population, China might have decided to use its population as the US did with its market. But the usage of moving tourists and fixed market are two quite different levels of punishments in terms of cruelty.

Hong Will the Chinese population be as effective as the US market as a weapon?

Lee Both China and the US must have concluded that it would. That's the reason China used the travel ban as its weapon, and the US warned China that it would take that as a low-level attack on its ally. The US must have feared the effectiveness of the weapon too.

Hong Now I get it. As of now, about 130 million Chinese, which accounts for about 10 percent of the entire Chinese population, are traveling to foreign countries each year, but when that percentage increases to around 30 percent, an average for developed countries, it can be used as an efficient weapon that could terrify other countries.

Lee Correct. For example, the majority of visitors to the ski resort in Hokkaido, Japan, are Chinese coming from southern China. They visit Hokkaido to enjoy the snowy landscape. If these Chinese tourists abruptly stop visiting Hokkaido, even Japanese government will have hard time pacifying the island's residents.

SIX GRAVE MISTAKES CHINA MADE IN THE LAST FIVE YEARS

Hong I understood that it was a big mistake for the Chinese government to ban Chinese nationals from traveling to Korea in retaliation for the deployment of THAAD on the Korean peninsula. I wonder what other mistakes the Chinese government made in the 2010s. And why did they make the mistakes?

Lee Let me talk about the background of those mistakes first. Around 2010, China surpassed Japan in total GDP, thereby replacing Japan as the world's second-largest economy. The United States, the world's largest economy under Obama administration since 2009 had been struggling to recover from the financial crisis that started in 2008. It was from this time that China made a series of mistakes. I believe their mistakes were triggered by the pride of China's replacement of Japan as the world's second largest economy. Plus, their overextended ambition to catch up with the United States contributed also because the U.S. at the time was in the whirlwind of financial crisis.

Hong A professor from Tsinghua University in China predicted that China's economy would overtake the United States' economy beginning around 2020 at a seminar that took place in Seoul in 2016. He probably meant it in terms of PPP (purchasing power parity).

Lee Perhaps because of such confidence, China made six critical mistakes within a short span of five years between 2013 and 2018. The Chinese like to refer to "100 years of humiliation" inflicted by Japan and the Western powers that began with the First Opium War in 1842 and ended with the founding of the People's Republic of China by Mao Zedong's China in 1949. But those six mistakes they made in a short span of just 5 years will remain in their memories for as long as the "100 years of humiliation."

Hong Were the mistakes that serious? And what were those serious six mistakes?

Lee They were serious mistakes because they united the U.S., European powers and Japan into a single front against China. Let me explain those six mistakes in chronological order.

Hong I will keep quiet until you finish your explanation. I want to focus on what you say.

Lee I'm just going to list actual events in a chronological order.

First, it is about the "Spratley Islands," which China reclaimed on international waters in the South China Sea in 2013. The Spratley Islands became the cause of conflict with surrounding countries as well as the United States over its territorial ownership and commercial shipping and fishing disputes. Besides, even though Xi

Jinping promised Obama that China would not deploy military facilities on the islands, China broke that promise and built military facilities including runways in 2017. The world was astonished at the blatant arrogance of China. Moreover, surrounding countries could not acknowledge the ownership of the South China Sea as claimed by China, because if the world acknowledged China's ownership of the sea, China will occupy more than 90% of the South China Sea.

The second is about "Made in China 2025", which China declared in 2015 as a sort of master plan for their national development. The main point of this policy was that, by 2025, China will become the global leader in high-tech fields including semiconductor, robotics and artificial intelligence. This was an open statement about their determination to bring down the US into a second-class power, a country that is up to its neck with astronomical $21 trillion national debt but somehow manages to remain as the leader in the high-tech industry.

Hong When China declared "Made in China 2025" in 2015, China was far behind in those three areas. Was there any basis for them to have such confidence at the time?

Lee It was revealed later, but China seems to have been developing plans to buy out companies that owned technologies that they needed or forcing companies to give them technologies by promising them access to the vast Chinese market just like China has been doing all this time. In fact, in 2018, China tried to take over an American high-tech company through a Singapore-based company but failed due to interception by the US government.

The third is the measures China took when THAAD was deployed in Korea in 2016. I've already explained about this case previously, so I won't repeat it here.

The fourth mistake was China's decision to remove presidential term limits from its constitution in early 2018. That means the current

Chinese leader Xi Jinping can stay in power indefinitely as long as the domestic situation allows it and it is necessary to achieve national goals. This is the direct opposite of the message Deng Xiaoping had left for his successors when he said, "Power should not be given to a small number of people for a long time."

Hong Why would the Chinese leaders accept measures that would allow one leader to stay in power for an indefinite term?

Lee It seems to me that their vengeance for the past "100 years of humiliation" must have clouded their rational judgement.

Hong Indeed, I agree that, if human rationality and vengeance clashed in a do-or-die battle, vengeance is more likely to win.

Lee At any rate, in the case of China, vengeance seems to have been winning over rationality during the five years between 2013 and 2018. China seems to have been captivated by their delusional dream of overtaking the US and becoming the world's strongest economic power and the hegemon of the world, so that China can bring the entire world under the influence of the great new China for China to settle scores with Japan and Western super powers for their 100 years of humiliation.

Hong Do you mean the Chinese leaders simply and utterly were not aware of the deep-seated uneasiness, distrust and nervousness of the leaders and the intellectuals of the world over China's possible prolonged one-man rule?

Lee Obviously they were not. The leaders and intellectuals of the Western countries who had previously revered the ancient culture of the Chinese civilization, the basis of which is capable of improving or even replacing the basis of Western political system, might have come to the opposite conclusion. That is that the Chinese leadership was "nothing more than an illegitimate offspring of Communism, trying to reinstate the tradition of the long dictatorship of Stalin, the legitimate heir of Karl Marx' Communism." It is a common sense that no country in the world will allow themselves to be degraded into a tributary state of the modern day Chinese emperor, or to be more specific, a Chinese megalomania leader we know as Xi Jinping.

Hong What was China's fifth mistake?

Lee The fifth was the frequency and timing of North Korea-China summit meetings in Beijing, arranged by Xi Jinping. They didn't meet each other for the six-year period between 2011 when Kim Jong-un succeeded his father upon his death and 2018 when they had three successive meetings in February, March and June. These three summits were significant in their frequency and their timing. February meeting took place after Kim Jong-un expressed his intention to comply with complete denuclearization after having been seriously pressured by the United Nations economic sanctions. The summit in March took place at a time when a summit with the United States was being planned, and the summit in June took place just one week after a North Korea-US summit.

Hong I guess Xi Jinping must have sensed the urgency of the situation, because he didn't meet Kim Jong-un at all for six years after Kim rose to power until all of a sudden, he had meetings with him three times in just half a year. Trump must have been aware of Xi Jinping's influence over Kim Jong-un.

Lee Of course, he did. Furthermore, Trump didn't try to hide his concern that Xi Jinping might have been a bad influence over Kim Jong-un.

Hong Are you saying that Trump had a motive behind his public display of concern about Xi Jinping's bad influence over Kim?

Lee By doing that, Trump effectually delivered a message that said, "Don't be so ridiculous. China accounts for over 90% of the North's trade but you cannot control the North!" Chinese leaders took notice of it, and I'm sure they realized that Trump was completely different from former US presidents.

Hong Did China have an opportunity to treat Trump differently after that?

Lee They frittered away the opportunity while they were busy weighing the possibility of Trump's impeachment, and appraising the mixed outcome of the U.S. mid-term elections. Trump eventually pulled out the bombshell tariff card. In this way, he branded China as a strategic competitor economically and as a systemic rival politically. In terms of the image seen from the perspective of advanced Western countries, China ended up with serious and irreversible damages.

The sixth mistake was the tit-for-tat policy of China in response to the US government's decision in 2018 to impose 25 percent tariffs on almost $34 billion worth of Chinese imports. In 1974, US President Carter passed the Trade Act of 1974. Section 301 of this trade act is about protecting the intellectual property rights of United States industry, and the main content of the section authorizes the US President to "impose trade sanctions such as duties on products imported from countries that are judged to have violated trade agreements."

Ever since China became a member of WTO in 2001, China has seldom allowed wholly-owned local subsidiaries of foreign companies for Chinese domestic markets. This Chinese policy is equivalent to mandated sharing of intellectual properties of those foreign companies with local partners. Even though this kind of "forced transfer of intellectual properties" is a violation that is so apparent that you cannot dispute it, China responded with a tit-for-tat policy of imposing tariffs on the US imports.

If China had agreed, in principle, to amend its domestic laws that don't allow a wholly-owned subsidiary of foreign firms, China's hegemonic policy would not have been exposed to the world and no united front of Western super powers against China might have emerged. And also Trump would not personally have been able to round up the support of American constituents.

These are the six major mistakes that China has made, and it is certain that these mistakes will make China lose the momentum of its rapid growth streak that has continued for 16 years since China joined WTO in 2001. It is even thinkable that China may experience "lost 10 years", or possibly "lost 20 years," just like Japan experienced.

Even if such a case becomes a reality, China should accept it as the consequence of its own deeds and move towards the courageous reestablishment of its domestic political structures. When China joined WTO, it made an implicit promise to the world: democratization of Chinese politics and the establishment of a market-driven economy.

LIMITS OF CHINA REVEALED THROUGH THE DEPLOYMENT OF THAAD ON THE KOREAN PENINSULA

Hong Will China continue to be arrogant? China's retaliatory response to the deployment of THAAD in Korea alarmed all countries around the world, because China clearly showed how it can deal a serious blow to other countries by using its population as a weapon. The tourism infrastructures cannot be diverted easily for other purposes and the replacement of tourists from one country to the other is a time-consuming process.

Lee China will be cautious from now on, because the United States sent a stern official warning to address the arrogance of China. It is beyond my imagination that Chinese leaders could be so recklessly arrogant. The Chinese leaders that I know have never gone that low. What happened to them?

Hong I don't think I am qualified to answer that question. But I can relay to you what I've recently heard from a professor who is familiar with recent American politics.

Lee I'd appreciate that.

Hong I can summarize his observation as follows:

"China's arrogance did not happen overnight. It had continuously nurtured for the last decade from 2008 to 2017. It is to note that the year 2008 was marked by the financial crisis that originated from subprime mortgage loans in the US, exposing the vulnerability of the US economy, and the year 2017 was marked by the end of Obama Administration, under which not a single person was sent to jail for having destroyed the American middle class."

"Obama is just an idealist who was elected

to the presidency supported by the strong organizational and financial powers that include major news media outlets that were controlled by a group of plutocrats, whose wealth has increased exponentially through the Asian financial crisis in 1998. Obama was nominated as the Democratic presidential candidate, all because the plutocrats who became strong by then decided that it was high time they elect a president of their choice.

"Even though these plutocrats committed a cruel crime when they destroyed the future of Americans and their families, Obama exonerated them and provided them with additional bail-out money which ultimately added to the US national debts."

"It was something that would never have happened if labor unions or the press were able to function as they were supposed to, but the labor unions grew so weak since the Reagan administration, and most media outlets were controlled by plutocrats when Obama took office."

"The Obama administration's succeeding administration will end in 2025, assuming two-term presidency of eight years. Many people including the Chinese leaders must have been convinced that Hilary Clinton, the presidential candidate chosen by plutocrats, would win the election and become the successor of Obama."

"That's the reason Chinese leaders became determined to seize the hegemony of the world during the 16-year period of two American presidencies of Obama and Hillary between 2009 and 2025. Subsequently, China planned a prolonged one-party rule with Xi Jinping as its leader in 2013 and declared to the world its policy of "Made in China 2025" in 2015, which in effect was their official manifesto about China becoming the world hegemon by 2025. And then China's other arrogances like the issuance of travel ban ensued."

This is a rough summary of his observation. I hope it helped.

Lee It's a convincing reasoning. It seems like '2025'

part of China's "Made in China 2025" is finally explained.

Part IV

ECONOMIC WAR BETWEEN THE US AND CHINA, AND THE PATH TO DENUCLEARIZATION OF THE KOREAN PENINSULA

IMPACT OF "MADE IN CHINA 2025" ON KOREA

Hong You gave me a full account on how the United States responded to China's declaration of "Made in China 2025," but you haven't told me how it could have affected Korea.

Lee Korea was the country that was supposed to get hit the hardest. You can even say that the fate of the Korean economy was sealed the minute China declared "Made in China 2025" in 2015. If the advanced high-tech technologies of Korea, such as Samsung's semiconductor technology and Hyundai Motor's engine technology that have spearheaded the economic growth of Korea are forced to be transferred to China, it will be a matter of time that Korea will be downgraded to a peripheral tributary state of China.

Hong But China's "Made in China 2025" is not meant to target Korea, is it?

Lee The target of the policy was advanced countries of the world, particularly those whose economy is heavily dependent on high-tech industry. The first victim should have been Korea, because of close trade relationship between two countries. However Trump's surprising election victory and his subsequent trade war with China helped Korea avoid the calamity miraculously.

Hong Samsung and Hyundai could just stay away from the Chinese market to avoid problems, couldn't they?

Lee Then both Samsung and Hyundai would lose their global competitiveness. For example, there are many major American high-tech companies whose revenue is heavily dependent on the Chinese markets. They include Qualcomm, a company where about 65 percent of its revenue is from Chinese market; Micron, 55 percent; Intel, 40 percent; and Boeing, 25 percent.

Hong The power of the market is terrifying. Besides, unlike the United States, Korea has a significant dependency on China particularly in terms of trade volume and trade surplus, doesn't it?

Lee China is Korea's largest trade partner, and the same applies to trade surplus. If Samsung Electronics and Hyundai Motors stay away from the Chinese market to avoid transfer of their technologies, the Chinese government may pressure the Korean government to make the technology transfer happen. It is quite possible in consideration of the Chinese government's action on Lotte in response to the deployment of THAAD on the Korean peninsula.

Hong What action did the Chinese government take on Lotte?

Lee The Chinese government, for providing Lotte-owned golf course as a site of THAAD installation, punished Lotte for alleged violation of minor fire safety ordinances to the point of total closing of Lotte stores. And Hyundai Motors had to close the factory in China because Chinese local parts suppliers to Hyundai Motors altogether stopped deliveries of auto parts on the pretense of fund shortage.

Hong China must be looking down on Korea. China couldn't have done the same to Western Powers, could it?

Lee China's extraordinary harshness to Korean companies may be due to Korean government's somewhat submissive attitude to a certain extent. However the arrogance of China seems to be more universal in that Chinese government blatantly built reclaimed islands on international waters in the South China Sea. It seems more likely that Chinese government has been captivated by the desire to flex their muscles with the backing of enormous population and wealth under its control. Under those circumstances, I'm not sure if such a small country like Korea means anything at all to the Chinese.

Hong Is China much different from a corporation that

strictly follows directions from the commanding post, known as the Communist Party?

Lee China is equivalent to a large corporation that hires 1.4 billion employees and owns as an asset Continental China with Chinese communist party as its management team. And the Central Politburo of the Communist Party which is a group of 25 members is equivalent to its board of directors, of whom nine Politburo members holding a seat on the Politburo Standing Committee are executive directors.

Hong About a quarter century ago, the United States must have proactively brought China out to the global stage under certain expectations of China's role in the international community.

Lee China was admitted to WTO in 2001 under the implicit condition that China would pursue a market-driven economy, abide by the international laws and maintain the universal standard of human rights. But for the last 18 years till today in 2019, the Communist Party of China has been virtually controlling over 60% of major corporations. Furthermore, the "Made in China 2025" policy that China announced in 2015 is a form of a manifesto of China's intention to officially strengthen the state capitalism structure where state and economy are not separated, as China has always been.

POSSIBILITY OF THE NORTH'S DENUCLEARIZATION AND THE ITS STAKES ON THE US, CHINA, AND RUSSIA

Hong Now, shall we move our subject to the north of the Korean Peninsula? In terms of the size of economy alone, per capita income of North Korea is one-twentieth of South Korea, and the population is only half of South Korea. That means, the economy of North Korea is just one-fortieth of South Korea at best. You can say it's equivalent to the economy of the city of Daegu and two to three surrounding industrial complexes combined.

Lee That's a good comparison. However, the size of economy set aside, North Korea has three facets of significance. First, North Korea has a geopolitical significance as a buffer zone between China, Russia and the United States. Secondly, North Korea is so close to South Korea that it can destroy South Korea to ashes even with conventional weapons. Third, North Korea has nuclear weapons and missiles that are classified as weapons of mass destruction.

Hong It seems we cannot talk about the North's missiles and nuclear development programs without mentioning Kim Jong-un. What kind of a man is he?

Lee A series of diplomatic and political actions that Kim Jong-un has taken after Kim Jong-il's death in 2011 was enough to draw attention of the world. Of all his actions, cruel political persecutions that he'd committed to strengthen his power, such as a summary execution of his power man uncle and the poisoning assassination of his half-brother in broad day light at the airport of a foreign country, seemed like stories you can find only in pulp fictions, revealing his personality. But it was the nuclear development program that he was most stubbornly obsessed with. In early 2018, he proposed denuclearization of the Korean Peninsula, but we don't know if he really meant it, or if it was just a stopgap measures in response to the US-led international pressure. But not many people would believe he truly meant to do it without expecting anything in return.

Hong Can you name one characteristic of Kim Jung-un's nuclear weapon development program, different from his father Kim Jong-il's?

Lee No doubt it is his intercontinental ballistic missile (ICBM) and nuclear warhead development program. A few years after he rose to power in 2011, a photo of Kim Jong-un with the map showing the trajectory of a ballistic missile to Washington from North Korea on the background was released, which is more like a cut from a comic book. But in 2016 to everybody's surprise, N.K. claimed a successful test of a hydrogen bomb and ICBM, as if a cut from a comic book became a reality.

Hong Did the international community accept N.K.'s claim as the fact?

Lee Fact or not, international community, particularly Washington was petrified by the claim. Even though China and Russia pretended to be proactively joining the U.N.'s decision to sanction N.K. in line with concerns over the proliferation of nuclear weapons and missile technologies, they could have been secretly rooting for Kim Jong-un, who is recklessly toying with nuclear weapons, and threatening the U.S. which is 400 times bigger in the size of economy.

Hong Do you really think so? Russia and China as permanent members of the UN Security Council are responsible for the security of the world, aren't they?

Lee The relative calmness of China and Russia and the hypersensitive reaction of the U.S. emanate from differences of their stakes in the N.K.'s nuclear capability. From the perspective of the U.S., it is not possible to accept North

Korea being a nuclear power in the first place, not to mention the N.K.'s capability to attack Washington with nuclear missiles. Washington knew that they could not afford to delay action any longer. But no easy solution was in their sight.

Hong Don't they have about a dozen powerful aircraft carriers on the ocean, waiting for the attack order from US President?

Lee Of course the U.S. has the military capability to instantaneously destroy North Korea's nuclear facilities, but Washington had to consider the possibility that the N.K.'s military counter-attack on South Korea, which may cost lives of millions of population in Seoul metropolitan area. Despite this danger, there was a reason not to delay the attack.

Hong What was the reason?

Lee It's the danger of the possible spreading of the N.K.'s nuclear and missile technology to Middle Eastern Muslim countries. For your reference, Israel destroyed a nuclear power plant in Syria that was under construction in 2007. And in 2008 a US intelligence report confirmed that North Korea's technology was involved in that nuclear power plant.

Hong That seems to prove how terrifying globalism can be, because the N.K.'s nuclear technology was passed so easily to Syria. Now shall we move on to Russia's position?

Lee Before talking about Russia's position, I want to make one comment concerning the U.S.'s bombing of North Korea. The U.S. should not bomb the N.K. not only for humanitarian reasons but also for the U.S.'s selfish reason.

Hong What is their selfish reason?

Lee The U.S. will be robbed of the final opportunity to recover from $21 trillion debt, if the U.S. will wage another war, which will be in all probability the most catastrophic in human casualties of all wars in history.

Hong Let's move to Russian perspective, please. It's an abominable horror to even think about it.

Lee Russia may tend to gloat over America's

entanglement in a nuclear threat from a tiny country whose economy is less than one-fortieth South Korea and one-four hundredth of the United States. Russia's attitude is understandable in consideration of their retrophilia of the golden days of Imperial Russia when Russia was under the reigns of Peter the Great and the German-born Empress, Catherine the Great, or the modern history of Soviet Russia when one third of the world was under the rule of Communism during the era of Stalin of the 20th century. It is absolutely natural for Russians to feel Russian Federation of the present era is being treated unfairly in the international community.

Hong I think I can relate to Russians' feeling about their current situation. The German-born Russian Empress Catherine the Great encouraged German peasants to emigrate to Russia to promote Russia's backward agriculture; later, the descendants of these German farmers immigrated to America to avoid political persecution and developed agriculture in the

U.S. Midwest; the beans produced by their descendants have been exported to China and contributing to meet China's big demand of pork; and now, the bean is at the center of the trade war between the United States and China. Interesting, isn't it?

Lee That's why people say history is more fictional than a fiction. Actually the United States had aggravated Russians' feelings by accepting the Soviet's satellite states as members of NATO after the fall of the Soviet Union in 1991. Furthermore, despite Russia's ownership of overwhelming number of nuclear weapons, Russians might have felt that they have not been duly respected because of the resource-dependent nature and the size of the Russian economy, about one-tenth of that of the United States. That is another reason why I think that Russians might be even enjoying watching North Korea whining to the United States like a little brat with their successful development of nuclear warhead and ICBM as a wild card.

Hong Then what about the position of China on this?

Lee From the perspective of China, the greater the North Korea's threat is to the United States, the more useful North Korea will be to China. China is convinced of the U.S.'s hesitancy in bombing North Korea's nuclear facilities because of the possibility of massive scale of South Korean casualties, and also of the U.S.'s full awareness of China's capability to control North Korea because of their trade relations, with China constituting over 90 percent of North Korea's international trade volume.

Hong So, the United States will try to avoid any activity harmful to its relationship with China, because of North Korea.

Lee Exactly. The reclaimed islands on the South China Sea and China's violation of the US intellectual property rights might have had something to do with it. In other words, China is taking a good advantage of its virtually exclusive right of access to North Korea.

Hong In that case, if Trump negotiates with Kim Jong-un in a face to face summit meeting, it will mean Trump is depriving China of its exclusive right of access to the North. It will be a good example of a diplomatic dexterity, personally and nationally, for him.

Lee What do you mean by personally?

Hong There was a saying in U.S. political circles of "kick the can down the road" to describe the past U.S. presidents' handling of the N.K's nuclear program. Trump had simply "no road to kick the can down". As a Christian and as a human being, Trump would have wanted to save Korean Christians as a Christian himself and fellow human beings as a human being himself from the disastrous massacre caused by massive radiation leak that would follow the bombing of North Korea.

Lee I see your point. Probably that's the reason Trump tried to mollify Kim Jong-un with a proposal of a summitry. This is an instantaneous upgrade of the status of Kim, the head of the worst failed state, to that of Trump, the head of the super power of the world.

Hong I think that's why Trump proudly waved Kim Jung-un's letter in front of TV cameras, as if he was pleading to American people, "Don't push me to go for the bombing. I will somehow negotiate with Kim Jong-un for him to give up his nuclear program."

Lee I see Trump had a good reason for his childish behavior.

Hong Now, starting from late 2016, we witnessed an abrupt change in attitudes of both China and Russia, proactively joining in the movement to sanction North Korea in accordance to the UN resolution of 2016. What do you think was the real reason for that?

Lee When North Korea claimed that it was a hydrogen bomb, not an atomic bomb that they had successfully tested in July 2016, their claim posed serious new threats to China and Russia for two reasons. One is that even though hydrogen bombs have never been used before, they are far more destructive than atomic bombs. The other is that it is easier to downsize the bomb, making it easier to be built into a warhead of long-range missiles. For these reasons, it is not only a threat to China to have a tiny neighbor to possess such monstrous weapons, but also there is a danger of miniaturized derivative weapons slipping into the hands of minority ethnic groups within their own country such as the Tibetans and the Uighur people. In that sense, Russia was in a similar situation with the Chechen independence activists. That was one of the reasons China and Russia proactively participated in the high-level UN sanctions of North Korea, proposed by the United States in December 2017.

NORTH-US SUMMIT FOR DENUCLEARIZATION

Hong Your theory about Kim's provocative, yet childish "Washington Bombing" scenario amusing somewhat the leaders of China and Russia is convincing, because these two countries have had grievances against the US's frequent exercise of the military power around the world since the fall of the former Soviet Union in 1991. In line with that, it is not unthinkable that China and Russia contributed, intentionally or unintentionally, to funding North Korea's nuclear program, with China aggressively importing coal from North Korea, and with Russia hiring a large number of North Korean workers for their Far East development projects.

Lee I don't have a solid proof to corroborate it, but in case of Russia, it might have gone one step further. The Russian government might have ignored scientists of the former Soviet Union, who were nostalgic for Communism, secretly participating in or consulting North Korea's nuclear and missile development projects.

Hong Your conclusion is that the danger of North Korea's hydrogen bomb technology making its way into the hands of Chinese and Russian ethnic insurgents, and also the possibility of North Korea, a tiny state with the hydrogen bomb and long-range missile technology becoming an uncontrollable threat itself are the reasons why the UN resolution in December 2017 was unanimously approved by all the permanent members of the United Nations Security Council including China and Russia. And all of a sudden, China and Russia started to cooperate in all earnest on sanctioning North Korea.

Lee You summarized it well. Their cooperation must have been a tremendous shock to Kim Jong-un. Even though he was ruling North Korea with an iron fist, he would not have any solution to appease the people who will be suffering from serious economic hardships that were soon to follow the UN sanctions. On top of that, Kim Jong-un would have felt an unimaginable sense of betrayal by China. That's the reason Kim Jong-un came out with the "denuclearization of the Korean Peninsula" card. His non-nuclear policy would have sounded persuasive to North Korean residents as well because it just so happened that a newly elected South Korean administration was leaning more towards pro-North than previous administrations. Later, when the peace mood was in its climax following the South-North summit and later the US-North summit in Singapore, China, startled at this rapidly changing situation, stepped right into the Korean Peninsula issue by inviting Kim Jong-un to Beijing just one week after the Singaporean Summit.

Hong Did Xi Jinping really need to openly get himself involved in the situation at such a sensitive time, taking the risk of incurring suspicion from Trump?

Lee I think that the intervention of Xi Jinping was inevitable from the standpoint of China. Considering Trump's unpredictable diplomatic style, even an agreement to open a US embassy in Pyongyang was a definite possibility. Then, the US Marines in charge of the security of the US embassy signifying the presence of US troops in Pyongyang would create a situation where China is facing the US troops just across the North Korea's border. This must have been the worst scenario China could not accept at any cost. Furthermore, China had always believed that denuclearization of North Korea will gain the withdrawal of the US troops from South Korea at a minimum. And North Korea's TV news coverage of the US-North Korea summit with fervor and enthusiasm must have shocked China's leadership.

Hong I clearly remember watching on TV news a female anchor hilariously mentioning Trump's kindness, showing his "Beast (nickname for Trump's vehicle)" to Kim Jong-un. By the way, somebody said that Trump's gesture of extraordinary kindness was motivated by the high-quality REEs buried near Jeongju-si, North Pyeongan Province in North Korea.

Lee I also have read an article in the American magazine Forbes about North Korea's mineral resources such as REEs.

Hong Did the article mention anything about the estimated value of the REEs buried in North Korea?

Lee I remember it was around $5 trillion. It was such a big number that I could hardly believe it.

Hong Considering Apple's market capitalization of $1 trillion, it means North Korea has five Apple Corporations buried under its ground in North Pyeongan Province or 20 Samsung Electronics.

Lee It is such a dreamlike story that I have hard time believing it. However, if the worth of North's

REEs is at least $1.5 trillion, we would not have to worry about the cost of reunification, because the amount is almost equivalent to GDP of South Korea.

ECONOMY WAR BETWEEN THE US AND CHINA AND THE PROSPECT OF THEIR RELATIONS

Hong How will the US-China relationship develop in the future? The tone of the most press coverage of the US-China summit that happened on December 1, 2018 during the G20 annual meeting was that the summit ended in a temporary truce of the trade war.

Lee Future US-China relations are truly unpredictable. It's neither a simple economic issue nor a complex ideology or hegemony issue.

Hong To predict the US-China relationship, wouldn't it be helpful to review the series of events from the US presidential campaign in 2016 to the G20 meeting in Argentina in 2018?

Lee Would you do that, please?

Hong I will try to summarize the events, based on my conversation with Dr. Kim and some follow-up information I picked up later. Plus, what you have explained to me so far.

In 2016, as a presidential campaign promise, Trump advocated the use of the US pressure on China for China to apply serious pressure on North Korea into giving up their nuclear program. And as a tool to pressure China, Trump cited the US trade deficit with China of about $ 300-$500 billion a year.

At that time, there was a group within the Trump election campaign camp who strongly insisted on the need to contain China, claiming, "China will become the hegemon of the world unless it is contained within the next five years, or no later than 10 years." This group recommended treating the North Korean issue as a subset of China issue for the hegemony war. They asserted that US bombing cannot be a solution because of the possibility of creating millions of South Korean casualties in the Seoul metro area. Thus, they radically claimed that a trade war with China has to be an economy war, because it also involves the solution of a nuclear threat by North Korea.

In early September 2018, Trump revealed a plan to expand the range of import tariffs from the current $ 50 billion worth of Chinese imports to $200 billion worth of Chinese imports as soon as a public-comment period ends. Later on, he even went on to say that he could impose tariffs to over $ 250 billion worth of remaining Chinese imports. On September 17, the US announced that the tariffs would go into effect at a rate of 10 percent for $200 billion worth of Chinese imports and that the rate could be increased to 25 percent by January 1, 2019. It became indeed more than just a tariff war. It was the level of an economy war, involving North Korea's nuclear threat to the U.S. as the important subset of China issue in the hegemony war.

Lee Are you insisting that North Korea's nuclear

program greatly contributed to this transition from a trade war to an economy war between the U.S. and China?

Hong Yes, absolutely. And furthermore North Korea's nuclear program besides transitioning from trade war to economy war also elevated later to a systemic rivalry between Democratic Capitalism and State Capitalism. My argument will sound more convincing to you if you think about the sequence of seven major developments as follows.

First, North Korea's hydrogen bomb test in September 2017 posed a threat to China and Russia, not only because of power of hydrogen bomb but also because of the easiness of downsizing the bomb. In December 2017, UN Security Council Resolution 2397 (UNSCR 2397) was unanimously passed in the aftermath of North Korea's ICBM test.

Second, in the year 2018, when China and Russia proactively participated in the UN's resolution to impose sanctions on North Korea, Kim

Jong-un had no other alternative but to declare denuclearization of the Korean Peninsula under the pretext of following the "teachings left by his ancestors," and tried to reach out to the United States through the newly-established, pro-North South Korean administration. In this process it was clearly revealed to the world that China's serious sanctions on North Korea was all that was required for North Korea's expression of intention for denuclearization. The whole thing reminds me of a scene from the movie Godfather.

Lee What do you mean? Which scene are you talking about? I'm curious because I've watched the movie several times.

Hong In the movie, the godfather told Tom Hagan: "Tattaglia's a pimp. … But I didn't know until this day that it was Barzini all along." What he meant was that it was a man named Barzini, the mediator of the peace treaty, who masterminded his son's murder.

Lee I should watch the movie again. Please continue.

Hong Third, after Kim Jong-un's declaration of his

decision on denuclearization, the South-North summit was held at Panmunjom and then finally the US-North Korea summit in Singapore on June 12, 2018. A week later on June 19th, Xi Jinping invited Kim Jong-un to Beijing for their third summit and shortly afterward, China's sanctions against North Korea seemingly significantly relaxed, rendering North Korea less committed to following up on its promise to denuclearize.

Fourth, it was around this time the Secretary of State's visit to North Korea was announced and canceled just a day after the announcement. Soon after, Trump tweeted on Twitter, "After solving the problem with China first...." This tweet was an official declaration that he was going to solve North Korea's nuclear issue as a subset of China issue through an economy war, instead of a trade war, with China.

Fifth, around September 2018, the US Secretary of Defense released the US Department of Defense investigation report on China's retaliations against the deployment of THAAD on the Korean Peninsula, originally triggered by North Korea's missile capability. The report accused China of having used its foreign tourists, as a low-level attack on US allies. This was the first sign of branding China as a 'strategic competitor', upgraded from an 'economic competitor'.

Sixth, this branding for China as a 'strategic competitor' brought world attention to "Made in China 2025" program, China announced in 2015, as a hidden attention of China for the world hegemony of 'State Capitalism'. The forced transfer of advanced technologies of the Western world to local Chinese partners for an access of the vast market of China will eventually make China outpace Western world in chip design, robotics, and artificial intelligence. And once China becomes the leader in those fields, China will easily seize the hegemony of the world.

Seventh, if this happens, China can claim that State Capitalism defeated Democratic Capitalism in an ideological war, just as Capitalism won over Communism in 1991. Furthermore, towards the end of 2018, the "Forum on China-Africa Cooperation (FOCAC)" was successfully held in Beijing with almost all countries of African Continent participating. This is a clear sign of China's open promotion of 'State Capitalism' over 'Democratic Capitalism' utilizing 'One Belt One Road' initiative. China might have sensed that 'State Capitalism' should be an attractive system to leaders of developing countries who tend to dream of prolonged one-man rule. Anyway this event was an undisputed signal for the start of the era of 'Systemic Rivalry' between Western world and China.

Lee By the way, do you think these African leaders might be attracted to this Chinese system because of their dream of staying in power for an indefinite term?

Hong They may be attracted more by the sustainable and rapid economic growth the Chinese model has demonstrated for a prolonged time. And also that the Chinese model will be more appealing to people of Africa, a majority of whom belong to the low-income class.

Lee Then, it would not be impossible for this Chinese model to replace the models of advanced Western countries.

Hong If China keeps recording rapid economic growth, China's system in which a one-party dictatorship can remain in power for an infinite term can win. But now that the hidden intention of China has been exposed to the world by "One Belt One Road" initiative, "Made in China 2025" policy and especially by North Korea's nuclear program, it now became impossible to replace the advanced Western model.

Lee Why is China's rapid economic growth not possible now?

Hong In order for China to sustain continuous economic growth, China has to develop technology-intensive industries because China's manufacturing industries are losing their competitiveness to the so-called TPP countries including Vietnam due to higher wage level. However, in case of technology-intensive industries of mainly so-called 30/50-Club member countries, they will not concede their domestic high-tech markets to China. This will be especially true after the Western countries' relations with China deteriorated from a mere 'Trade War' to a 'Systemic Rivalry'.

Lee China may be faced with Chinese version of the "lost 10 years" or even "lost 20 years". "China Bashing" might have started already because at the end of December 2018, Apple decided to make their next model at a factory in India. It's like a flare that signaled the "China Bashing" into the air in view of the entire world. In the final analysis, North Korea's nuclear program played a key role in changing a trade balance issue with China into an existential issue for Western civilization.

Hong I agree with you. The US and other Western powers would have lost the opportunity to contain Chinese ambition if Kim Jong-un hadn't bragged about the North's hydrogen bomb or intercontinental ballistic missile and messed with it like a whiny little brat.

Lee Trump should be really grateful to Kim Jong-un. Actually, all citizens of the free world who oppose one-party dictatorship should be grateful to him for that.

Hong That is the capricious nature of history. Shakespeare said "Life is a tale told by an idiot" and likewise, I'd say history is also no more than a comedy written by fools. Anyway, Kim Jong-un should be proud of this accidental feat for humanity and I wish the Empire of the Kim Dynasty now disappears into political oblivion forever.

Lee I'm with you. Three generations of the Kim Dynasty has given too much suffering to North Korean residents for the last 70 years. A prominent scholar from a Western country often cites South and North Korea to prove that ethnicity has no causal effect on economic development, because South Korea is an epitome of the highest success while North Korea, a case of a tragic failure.

Hong There is one question that keeps lingering in my mind. Why on Earth did China act so arrogantly and so impatiently since Xi Jinping took power in 2012? Was he obsessed with the idea of reviving the golden days of the Ming Dynasty, China's last native dynasty?

CHINA'S GROWTH ENGINE AND POTENTIAL

Lee He might have been. In the early 15th century, the Ming Dynasty was a powerful Han Chinese Empire that once accounted for half of the world GDP at its prime time. Ming was clearly a superpower stronger than today's America, a country that accounts for less than a quarter of the world GDP today. Therefore, China's great yearning for that past glory is not to be criticized. Realistically, China's GDP being now 70 percent of the US GDP, China longs to become the world's top economic superpower replacing the United States in the next decade or so and to become the absolute superpower of the world as the Ming Dynasty once was, no later than 2049.

Hong Does the year 2049 have any special significance?

Lee Sure it does. The year 2049 marks the 100th anniversary of the founding of the People's Republic of China (PRC) by Mao Zedong in 1949. China is probably planning to get their sweet revenge for the "100 years of humiliation" by becoming the world's strongest superpower exactly a hundred years after the end of their "100 years of humiliation."

Hong Do you think there is a possibility of China getting that sweet revenge?

Lee There surely is a possibility. Well... let me take it back. I should have said there would have been a distinctive possibility unless and until America has aggressively tried to contain China as a 'strategic competitor' since early 2018 when so-called 'trade war' erupted.

Hong What if we presume that America has not tried to contain China?

Lee As of today, China's population is roughly four times the US population. In terms of national GDP, China will become even with the United States if China's per capita GDP equals one-fourth of that of the United States. At the moment, America's per capita GDP is $60,000, which is six times that of China's $10,000, but given the difference in economic growth rate between the two countries, China may overtake the US in terms of GDP by 2030. There is a Chinese scholar who openly claims that, in purchasing power parity (PPP), China will become the world's largest economy in 2020.

Hong China was such a poor country at the time of the Tiananmen Square incident in 1989. What was the reason China could grow so fast within such a short time? Back then, China's per capita GDP must have been less than one-fortieth of the United States.

Lee The little giant, Deng Xiaoping, can be rightfully called the father of modern China. He had such a great admiration for Park Chung-hee who was responsible for the modernization of Korea that Deng Xiaoping is called the best disciple of Park Chung-hee. After witnessing the successful hosting of the 1988 Seoul Olympic Games, he pushed forward with the establishment of diplomatic relations with Korea in 1992 despite strong opposition from North Korea. And after establishing diplomatic relations with Korea, Deng spearheaded an export-led economic development drive, following Park Chung Hee's footsteps.

Hong Why did he choose the Park Chung-hee model instead of an advanced country model?

Lee The essence of the Western advanced countries' development model was the exploitation of colonies between the 16th and the 18th century at the hands of imperialist nations. After accumulation of social capital through the exploitation of colonies (in case of America's 'residence colonialism', the exploitation of the indigenous people), Western advanced countries were able to equip themselves with six elements that were necessary for economic development, as identified by a historian from Harvard University.

Hong What were those six elements?

Lee They were Competition, Technical Revolution, Private Property, Modern Medicine, Consumer Society, and Work Ethics. If you apply these six elements to the Park Chung-hee model of Korea, competition corresponds to Korea's highly competitive college admission system; technical revolution to Korea's construction of modern-day factories with international loans; private property was already guaranteed in Korea; modern medicine existed by state-led medical education, anti-epidemic measures, and a healthcare system in Korea; consumer society was found overseas with Korea's export-led economic system; and work ethics corresponds to Korea's Saemaeul movement.

Hong Then, do you mean the Deng Xiaoping model was the same as the Park Chung-hee model?

Lee No. They differed in many ways. The "competition" part was similar, but in the case of the "technical revolution", the first stage of the international loans was done mostly by the Chinese expats. In the case of private property, even though land was owned by the state, private ownership of houses was allowed. In case of modern medicine, China already had a highly advanced medical education. With regards to consumer society, China mostly relied on overseas market, the United States in particular, like Korea did. And work ethics was naturally resolved by allowing the private ownership of houses.

Hong How did he resolve the restriction-of-freedom related problems that result from the one-party rule of the Communist Party?

Hong Deng Xiaoping might have thought that the restriction of freedom was a solution to a problem, instead of a problem to be solved. He is the one who brutally cracked down the Tiananmen Square protests in 1989. In fact, if we look back on modern history, you cannot find any underdeveloped country that succeeded in achieving a self-supporting economy while maintaining functioning democracy at the same time. Imperialist countries had tendencies to implant democracy on their colonies when they were ready to leave their colonies. Perhaps their hidden intention was not to allow their colonies to become their potential competitors.

Hong I wonder if China has been relying on the US market for too long and too heavily for the export market of their products. China's excessive surplus in trade with the US has led to a "trade war", and China's violation of the US intellectual property rights has emerged as a major issue between the US and China.

Lee Advanced Western countries usually set up three entry barriers to keep developing countries from entering into the class of advanced countries. The first is human rights issues, the second is intellectual property rights, and the third is brain drain of local technicians and engineers.

China effectively neutralized the first and third barriers by officially declaring human rights issue as internal issue and tightening regulations on the local factories of foreign companies. I think China might have taken the second barrier, intellectual property rights, lightly because it overestimated the power of the access to their domestic market. China ended up entrapping itself in this barrier.

Hong How did Korea resolve this second barrier, intellectual property rights, to join the class of advanced countries? I bet the advanced countries set up the same barrier on Korea as well.

Lee There were three reasons. The first reason was that, the United States allowed technologies to flow into Japan as its ally during the Cold War era of the 1960s and these technologies naturally made their ways into Korea in later years. The second reason is that the size of Korean economy could not be a threat to the United States, and the third reason is that large Korean corporations did not neglect on investing in R&D.

Hong Since you brought it up, can you go on and tell me how Korea overcame the first and third barrier problems? Suddenly I am curious about it.

Lee Regarding the first barrier, the human rights issues, Park Chung-hee was able to put it off by using the slogan of self-sufficient economy as a shield, and by the time the Park Chung-hee administration came to its end, the foundation of the Korean economy became strong enough to guarantee human rights. In the case of the third brain drain barrier, dynamic labor movements that followed the 1988 Seoul Olympics effectively discouraged foreign companies to set up factories in Korea solely to extort capability of local technicians and engineers.

Hong It may not have been planned in advance, but looking back, Korea has been so fortunate at every turn even though Korea had to go through a period of suffering. In that sense, I cannot help but root for China to wisely overcome the difficulties that it is faced with now and make a successful entry into the line of advanced countries.

EPILOGUE

As you may guess from the title of this book, I was inspired to write this book by the fact that Korea became a member of the 30/50 Club.

Of course, it is not guaranteed that Korea will keep its membership in the 30/50 Club forever: Korea can drop out of the Club at any time as Spain once did, and Korea will be able to maintain the current status of the 30/50 Club only when Korea becomes a member of the "40/50 Club" in the future.

Among the other club members, namely the US, Germany, Japan, Britain, France, and Italy, the three countries from the bottom of the rank are within close range for Korea to overtake them within the next 10 to 20 years. Korea is currently the leader of the world in many fields: Airport facilities including immigration procedures; public transportation system represented by subway facilities; universal medical insurance system; quality of citizen service by local government offices; and cutting-edge telecommunication networks. Moreover, once the "Kim Young-ran Law" is settled down, Korea will be at the top in the anti-corruption level of the officialdom.

Korea, once one of the poorest nations in the world as late as in 1961 becoming one of the most advanced countries in the world in less than 60 years—it is not easy to pinpoint the reasons. If I am allowed to express my personal opinion, these are the contributing factors: an extremely competitive college admission system built upon the idea of equality; a fair military service system; devoted faith in Christianity and Buddhism based on Confucianism; a fierce spirit of personal competition; and most importantly, the industrious work ethics. In addition, Korea's obsession for "first-class" might have played a significant role as well, especially in high-tech fields.

I don't think there is any special chart that Korea should follow from now on. Koreans just need to respond timely to changes and to overcome crisis when they arise as they have always done and never lose confidence in the process. Countries around the world are trying to learn the secrets of success from Korea. Britain, once acclaimed as a country where "the sun never sets" is trying to learn about secrets of success of Korea, a country that signed free trade agreements with many countries and secured advanced technologies, in the process of exiting European Union. If Korea doesn't expand, evolve, and bequeath to its future generations the secrets of success, it would be a crime of the worst kind.

1950
Cheonggyecheon
2018 Cheonggyecheon

Appendix

1. President Park's Last Words

2. President Park Chung-hee, His Dedication and Legacy

Preface

"On the evening of October 26 (1979) at 6 pm in the evening, His Excellency President Park Chung-hee[1] attended a dinner prepared by Central Intelligence Agency Director Kim Jae-gyu[2] at a CIA dining room in Gungjeong-dong. An accidental confrontation broke out between Director Kim and Security Services Director Cha[3] during dinner, and shot by a bullet fired by Director Kim, the President passed away around 7:56 pm on the evening of the 26th."

The above is the content of the official announcement made by the government on the evening that President Park Chung-hee died on October 26, 1979, eighteen years after he seized power as an army general through the 1961 coup d'état.[4]

According to later disclosure, Park Chung-hee died from the two bullets fired by the KCIA director (first bullet in the chest, second bullet in the temple), and attending the drinking party besides those included in the official government announcement were a celebrity singer,[5] a young model[6] and the Presidential Secretary.[7]

The safehouse where the party was held was inside the compound under KCIA control. At another safehouse, the KCIA director arranged a dinner for the Army Chief of Staff, attended by the director's assistant. This arrangement was seemingly to show to his subordinates that he had the backing of the Korean Army leadership as well as the American CIA.

It was later reported that the moment of Park Chung-hee's death occurred while the Presidential Secretary, who had attended the party with him, was transporting him to the Korean Armed Forces Capital Hospital.[8]

The first piece "President Park's Last Words" is a fictionalization of Park Chung-hee's thoughts in the form of a monologue, from the moment he was shot by the first bullet to his death. A very subjective piece, I wrote it imagining myself as Park Chung-hee before he breathed his last.

Anyone can play the part and write such a story. Were the content of such a story to display a completely opposite sentiment than what I have written, I would have no intention of refuting it.

The second piece "President Park Chung-hee, His Dedication and Legacy" contains articles on his executive accomplishments in different areas, published by five different journalists over five days in a daily newspaper during the national mourning period.

There may be many different opinions on Park Chung-hee's accomplishments, but one clear thing is that during the 18 years he held power, between 1961 to 1979, Korea advanced from being one of the poorest countries in the world to 28th place in total GDP worldwide. Truly, it deserves to be called a miracle.

Although it is a redundant point, 2019 marks the 40th anniversary of Park Chung-hee's death. In 2017, the 100th year after his birth, plans were made to issue a commemorative stamp, but for some reason it did not materialize. In case his spirit felt hurt, I hope the publication of this small book may give him even a little consolation.

Sang Hwa Hong

July 1, 2019

Appendix 1

President Park's Last Words

by Sang Hwa Hong
(Translated by Won-Jae Hur)

Around 7 pm on October 26, 1979, eighteen years after taking power through a coup, a drinking party is taking place inside a National Security Agency[1] safe house[2] in Gungjeong-dong next to the Blue House.[3] Those attending are the president, director of the Korea Central Intelligence Agency, director of the Security Service, Presidential Secretary, a celebrity female singer, and a young model.

Growing tipsy from the whisky the young model has been pouring, the president is listening to the sweet sound of the woman singing to the tune of her guitar.

When it rains I think of you

You who were always so quiet

Secretly hiding your pain of love

Crying for the one who left you...

The president closes his eyes, as if overcome by a sudden wave of intoxication. At that moment, in his mind appears an image of his wife, killed by an assassin's bullet at the August 15th Independence Day celebration.[4] He whispers quietly to himself,

"Young-soo![5] After you left me, the Blue House has become a prison. It's like everyone in that place, even our dog Bell, is watching me fighting the loneliness all by myself. I can't bear this loneliness. In a bedroom somewhere in the corner of the damp and dark Blue House, I would fall asleep on the sofa, thanks to the liquor I'd keep sipping, and when I would wake up in the middle of the night, I had to listen to the sound of the drooping tree branches outside shaking in the wind. That sound would pierce the cold silence and suffocating sense of emptiness and mercilessly draw

near me. That's no place for a human being to live. It's a place only for corrupt power and flattery, pretense and hypocrisy. I've lost the strength to fight. No, there is no need to fight. Because the person I want to show my struggle to is gone. That place is my prison, a cold prison where your memories are locked up. On nights when sleep refuses to come, I toil on, if only to hear the hot, thunderous applause of the voiceless masses. I try to picture their faces in front of me, thinking sleep will come if I hear their applause. But it was all futile. Even tonight I'll drink with these young women and go back to my bedroom in the Blue House. Sleep will not greet me then. Please don't scold me too much for being like this. I would ask you could see it simply as an impulsive foolishness of a lonely man who has lost his life partner and cannot even see his son[6] anymore.

"If I could storm out of this place right now, run to the Military Academy and see my boy.... I envy the life of a common man![7] If only my son could have been born to a common man.

"Ah, my son! When I saw you as a boy staring blankly into space after your mother's death, when I saw you

in the wide corridors of the Blue House and met your eyes filled with resentment toward me, when I stood behind you and looked at you asleep at your desk while studying, I tasted pain more terrible than if a thousand bullets were to shatter my heart. And I felt endless regret. That, long ago, I didn't fulfill as trivial a thing as going to a baseball game when you asked me. That I had yelled at you for squabbling with your sister. And then I realized it. That I loved you more than anyone else. But how can this father show his love when he has taken his young boy's mother from him?"

As the drinking party begins to ripen, an argument erupts between the Central Intelligence Agency director and Security Service director about how the protests in Masan and Busan are to be put down.[8]

"Your excellency, how can anything go right when we are working with a maggot like this!" yells the CIA director, pointing at the Security Service director. The next instant, the CIA director takes out a gun, aims at the Security Service director's chest, and pulls the trigger.

"Bang!"

"Chief Kim, why are you doing this, why are you doing this!" the Security Service director stutters as he staggers and stands up, waving his hands in front of him.

"What the hell are you all doing!" the shocked president yells from his seat.

"Bang!"

The CIA director puts the gun to the president's chest and pulls the trigger.

The President collapses on his side.

The Security Service director takes the opportunity to run away to the adjacent bathroom. The Presidential Secretary, the singer, and the model are panic-stricken and shaking with fear. The CIA director pulls the trigger again but when the gun misfires, he rushes out of his seat and runs out of the room. The clock points exactly at 7:40 pm.

His chin resting on his chest, the president cries out within himself:

"Uggh..., what pathetic sight is this? Ah, I am dying. I am dying as a rake.... And bitten to death by a crazy

dog that I raised myself…. I didn't expect my life would end like this…. It can't be. If the god of fate has even a sliver of compassion, he would not allow my life to end like this.

"God of fate! How a soldier dies seals his life, and if I can't meet a heroic death under fire in a battlefield with fellow soldiers, then let me adorn my end alone in a cold prison. If even that is too merciful, then let me finish my life in old age, taking the mare of illness as my last comrade-in-arms and recalling the memories of my youth.

"Ah, that I should die as a libertine…. This is a disgrace. An unbearable disgrace, a disgrace that will last forever. It is a curse. The worst curse, the cruelest curse that heaven can lay on me. Why must I suffer such shame and fate? Why me? For what reason…. Alexander met his death on the road to conquest, Caesar on the floor of the Senate, Napoleon on an isolated island in exile, and Hitler in a bunker. But I am dying like a rake between two young women at a cozy drinking party.

"Mmm… it feels like my gut is stiffening. The blood

in my body is gushing out. Rotten, worthless blood. Poisoned by wild ginseng and costly Western liquor. Too much ginseng has made my blood boil in my veins, and too much drink has dyed my thick blood with arrogance. Get out, get out, get out quickly now. Fresh blood can come in only when rotted blood has gone out.

"Our country's rotted blood, blood steeped in failure, cowardice, and subservience, I changed that to blood filled with youth and confidence. Farmland without straw-thatched houses, mountains covered with green forests, powerful fire burning in smelting furnaces, a lifeline crossing the country's fields and mountains, wide plains covering the sea…, they are the foundation for our nation's modernization and revival of our nation. I did all of it. What everyone said was impossible I achieved by my own strength. Empty-headed mutts in the markets frothed at the mouth and barked false 'freedom' with their drooling tongues. But did I not accomplish all these without wavering in the slightest…."

At that moment, the dead politicians who were

politically persecuted and suffered during his term appear before him in a vision. The sound of their voices rebuking him can be heard from far away.

"How can you, who should've never been born in the first place, show your face to the world, and bring shame to the people and make parents weep blood? What's the use of living in abundance in a world that's worse than a pigsty. Heaven will not forgive the sins your rabble committed. For a human being should live like a human being, in freedom…."

When the vision of the dead politicians disappears, the president yells at them.

"Freedom? What kind of freedom is the freedom you all are barking about? The freedom to become servile? The freedom to be scorned? The freedom to self-indulge? The freedom to be hungry? … You don't know what it means to be hungry. Do you know anything about my mother who put her belly under a pestle to abort me, so her child would not suffer from hunger? A

mother like that, her desperate heart is poverty.

"To put to sleep those reckless fools who cry out for false freedom only for their own advancement, I raised and surrounded myself with rabid dogs. Security Service director, Intelligence director… they are all crazy dogs. Of course, you all feared them. Didn't you perk up your ears and sway your tails…. That's not all. Didn't you hover around to ingratiate yourselves to them? In the end, they've bitten me too. I should have locked them up in a cage sooner…. I should have shoved them into a cage of intoxication, luxury, lust and sloth…. I had planned on catching them and locking them up at some point…. Failing to do it sooner has now become an eternal regret.

"What? I who destroyed democracy won't be forgiven? You who cry out for American-style democracy, who are filled with ideology of subservience, do you even know what that democracy means? It is poverty, self-indulgence, despair, and the opiate. Don't you remember the time when the daughters of the white-robed people[9] *became playthings to foreign men in this land and called local mistresses? What happened*

to our peninsula as a result? Didn't it become a sewer of prostitution? You will remember the time when the stench that flowed out of the sewer wore a mask called 'democracy', burrowed itself into the people's bodies, paralyzing what little pride and sense of shame remained, and corrupted sons of the land into pimps and daughters of the land into whores.

"21st century Asian Superpower! That is a peak that our people must capture, making whatever sacrifice that is necessary. Our naïve people, seduced by crazy words of madmen. I raised rabid dogs around me to protect them from you lunatics. Madmen fear only mad dogs. There is no other medicine.

"It was just another day when these rabid dogs were roaming around me. Suddenly, I saw them furtively hiding their tails, and I realized they were my enemies. They were soiled with corruption and greed. I knew then that everything I had tried to eliminate had swelled up by my very side and built a filthy forest of power. I made them turn their teeth on each other and kill one another. Because it was something only rabid dogs could do. Ah, but now I am the one bitten.... Who could

have imagined it."

The president clutches his chest as if he were in pain, and quietly continues his monologue.

"Ah, the pain is hitting my chest. There is a saying, 'The ability to lead is the ability to inflict pain on others while not feeling pain oneself'. Let me try bearing this pain, I have to bear it. I cannot die like this. I can't die like this and let Kim Il-sung[10] live his life. You bastard, you don't amount to a lard-filled pig! You bastard killed Young-soo! That I should die before Kim Il-sung....

"Ah, is there a woman more to be pitied than Young-soo? Young-soo! I did not understand love's meaning. Until you left my side. To me love was loneliness, love was guilt, and love was an absurd separation. An eternal separation, a separation that can never be mended here on earth, but that very separation awakened me to my love for you.

"Do you know what I thought when Kim Il-sung's bullet missed me and pierced your head? The only thought I had was that the show must continue,

because the curtains have gone up and the audience has gathered. I continued my performance, reading the celebration speech, and in my mind, rather than thinking of you undergoing surgery, I was pondering how I should act in front of the crowd, the camera, the government mutts, the rabid dogs.... Even at that moment, I was a trained actor who contemplates his next performance. As you know, Napoleon was a superb performer who knew how to speak and act in any place, before any crowd. He took the entire European continent as his stage, but even if my stage were only half of the Korean Peninsula, I tried to act like him. People are born with a need to admire heroes. So they search for a hero to worship until they die. A leader has to put on a performance, to become their hero, to satiate their hunger for hero-worship.

"I finished reading the speech, picked up your handbag and the single white rubber shoe left beside the chair you had been occupying just a few minutes ago, and I left the hall with a dignified look.

"When I got into the car, I saw the empty seat where you had sat. That seat where you had sat until we

arrived at the hall emptied my heart, so I closed my eyes. And I clasped your lone rubber shoe tightly to my chest and wept. Even then, I held my head rigidly straight. Do you know why I wept? Because I deplored the fate that forced me to put on an act while you were at the crossroad of life and death..., because I grieved over such a fate."

At that moment, the singer, pulling herself together, helps the president sit up from the floor where he had lain after the shot to his chest.

"Your Excellency, are you okay?" the singer asks.

"I'm okay," replies the president in a quiet voice, keeping his eyes closed.

"Are you sure you are okay?" the Security Service director asks after cracking the door slightly open and peeking out. The president lies in the woman's arms and recollects the recent past, from his wife's death up to now.

"The fragrant scent of the woman holding me is arousing my sense of smell. An image of a young

woman's naked body is drawing near to me. The body of a young woman lying down on her back, lifting her legs in the air.... I can see her small feet, soft legs hanging in the air, strong thighs to hold them up, her thin waist so easily breakable, and her powerful pelvis.

"And in the middle, the young woman's secret cavern, that secret place that makes a king throw away his crown, wages wars reeking of blood, makes the world's saints into sinners, and turns lowly men into heroes..., the secret place that freely gives birth to sinner and saint, commoner and hero, beautiful woman and ugly woman..., the secret place where all the world's whims dwell.... To that secret place I gave a part of my body, and fought with all my power to soothe my bone-deep loneliness.

"The edges of a woman's closed eyes tremble with pleasure, and the cries that break free from a woman's tightly shut lips graze my ears.

"Although just a momentary illusion, it was a haven for a lonely man, regardless of age. Nothing would replace it to soothe the loneliness. Maybe it's the excuse of an aging man left all alone, but I can't help it. Having

lost my companion and wandering in loneliness, it was my refuge, my solace. For just that moment, I could be free from all anguish."

Two minutes after the CIA director's bullet pierced the President's chest, the director enters the room again with a new gun in his hand. He fires at the Security Service director who is coming out of the bathroom. The Security Service director collapses. The Presidential Secretary cringes in the corner, shaking.

The CIA director walks up to the President. The singer and the model run out of the room in fear. The President continues his thought.

"Gunpowder's spicy scent. Pointing it before him, he takes his long stride toward me, with death, invisible and intangible, squeezing the air around me. Death that once lingered right in front of me and just missed me wore an angry expression on its face. But the death approaching me now is wearing a placid smile. The cold gunpoint drawing near me, and the smell of gunpowder pouring out of it...."

The CIA director places the gun on the president's head. He pulls the trigger.

"Bang!"

The president's brain is fatally injured. His soul is leaving his body. The Security Service director has stopped breathing. The Presidential Secretary, who was the Army Chief of Staff fetched two security guards into the room and they are moving the body of the still breathing president out of the room to take him to the Korean Armed Forces Capital Hospital near the Blue House.

The president's monologue continues.

"My soul is leaving my body and moving through the air. With quick speed, with a peaceful heart.... The clouds and fresh air that touch my soul, and with peace at heart, my soul takes a moment to stand still to look up. I can see a stone stairway that reaches down from the sky, hanging in the air. At the top of the stone stairway, I see a roofed old fortress. Many colored, many shaped clusters of clouds that flow over the stairs like kites swaying in the wind, it's like a beautiful

painting. How wonderful it would be to look down at the world from the top of those stairs! Yes, even from this place, let me look down on the world one last time….

"I can see the foot of Bukak mountain and the massive grounds of the Blue House. I can see three people hastily stepping out of a cozy two-storied house nearby onto the lawn. Among them, a strong looking figure bears a thin man on his back …. I see that it is my body where my soul dwelled for those 62 years that passed like a moment. Was my body really so pathetically thin and sickly? The flesh where my soul lived, withered by liquor and lust, bruised by anger, dulled by greed, discolored by wickedness…. Its appearance is so shabby that no one would feel pity for him, even if it were dumped in a gutter. Next time, if by god's mercy he offers a human body to my soul instead of a dog or a swine's, I will firmly reject it. Rather than the fragile flesh of a human being, I wish to be a beast that runs freely in the fields or mountains, looking for prey, until it becomes food for a stronger beast and leaves only its bones.

"I can hear beautiful music coming from the old fortress.

"Ah, there is someone coming down the steps. An old, white-haired man in a black robe and black gat[11] *and, behind him, a woman whose face I can't see, wearing mourning clothes…, who can it be? I can't see clearly with the clouds covering them. I suppress my frustration and direct my gaze downward.*

"On the ground below, they are moving my pitiful body, carried on someone's back, into my car. That worthless body that breathed my breath, ate my food, slept with my woman, and lived my life is a stranger that has nothing to do with me. My body lying crumbled over the secretary's knees in the backseat, it is dyeing Young-soo's seat red-black with its remaining blood, oblivious that the soul has left. Filthy blood! Get out, get out, don't leave a single drop, but leave the body, soak the seat, drench my car in blood, flood the safe house, and if any still remains, seal this evening in your blood forever. Seal it deeply in my blood, so that history cannot find it, and, above all, nothing will reach my son's and daughters' ears and eyes.

"Chief Secretary! General Kim! Why are you covering the open gun wound in that body with your

hand? Take it off immediately. I am begging you. General Kim! It's time for that body to leave. For 18 long years, that body has been dragged through mud fields of crisis, rainstorms of foreign powers, swamps of excess, and ice fields of cruelty. It is so utterly spent, it is useless now. What? It still has so much to do? No, that's not true. The country now has to go where the "spirit of the times" points. All it has to do is take that path. In the 1960s, the spirit of our time was to escape from absolute poverty, and it was "prevention of communism" and "self-reliant economy" in the 1970s. In the coming 1980s, "democracy," "democracy in prosperity" must be the new spirit of the times, and it will be "attainment of cultured globalized citizen's consciousness" for the 1990s, and "achieving advanced nation status" in the 2000s.

"What? I'm being too greedy? General Kim! You still don't get it. Fifty years is plenty to become an advanced nation. If we can't get there in fifty years, we will never get there. Do you know how many countries run aground at the threshold of gaining advanced nation status? On the other hand, look at Japan. Within fifty

years of the Meji Restoration, it was able to go from a backward country to a nation equal with the Western powers. My days as a cadet in the Japanese Army Academy convinced me of something. That is, if Japan can do it, we can do it better. General Kim! Please tell this to our young people.

"General Kim! Brother Kim! Don't shed any tears. Don't look at the pitiful body on your knees and cry. What is so precious about that pathetic body that you shed tears over? As a soldier, a husband, a father, that body has lived a filthy life. A soldier who should die in gunfire next to his comrades is now dying a cowardly death, caressing young women at his side and bleeding from a subordinate's bullet. He let his kindhearted wife die from an assassin's bullet in front of the camera with thousands of people watching. As a discarded rake who has left his young children all alone and a shameful father who has brought upon himself a violent death, that body is now ending a treacherous life.

"General Kim! Chief Secretary! You still can't stop yourself? Take that filthy body and go right back into the Blue House. Lay it down on my second-floor bedroom,

blow it up so that there's no trace of my body, and then tell the people. Tell them that the President beloved by the people was sacrificed to an explosive hidden by an enemy on the night of October 26, 1979, leaving the world at the age of 62."

The President falls silent for a moment, then suddenly turns his head and glares at someone.

"What? Who should be my successor? Chief Secretary! Have no worries. Power is a filthy nymphomaniac, she will find the bosom of the strongest, most violent, most merciless to flirt with him. She will lie in his arms, and with fake moans, bewitching voice, sweet whispers, she will gather his jism bit by bit into her secret place and make him weak. Then she will drip the semen, rotted in her deep cavern, into the mouth of those who will put their tongues on her fetid spot.

"What? I shouldn't have done Yushin?[12] *Chief Secretary, General Kim! Why are you so soft? Did you even imagine what would have happened if we didn't do it? I saw through the people who directly*

witnessed America's defeat in Vietnam, especially cunning intellectuals and the intentions of opportunistic businessmen. Thinking Korea's next to fall to communism, the intellectuals quickly rack up points with Kim Il-sung, and the salesmen wait to grab their loot and flee abroad at an instant!

"You don't know. The deviousness of pseudo-intellectuals! The democracy they promote is just a show. Their real desire, what they are really prepared for is enjoying privileges in an ivory tower even if it's under Kim Il-sung! Ah, my heart feels like it will burst. When I imagine the world where naïve youths will have their noses hooked by their treacherous rakes and mistakenly dragged here and there..., my heart, my heart feels like it will tear apart.

"What? We still should have ended Yushin sooner? You are right about ending it. I also never had any intention of continuing it at all. But it was not the right time. General Kim, Chief Secretary! Look back on everything we have accomplished over the last seven years of Yushin. Independent self-defense was firmly established? Yes, you are right. We got rid of the bad

habit of wanting to put our defense in foreign hands. But that's not all. If we look at economic progress, that's not even comparable.

"What? Numbers don't mean that much? Hold on, how does someone who spent his life as a general say something so old-fashioned? I had something I wanted to tell the people: 'Abstract words are politicians' tricks'. Only numbers are true.

"Do you know what changes happened in the last seven years of Yushin? What? You don't need to know about something so minor as numbers? That is completely wrong-headed. You have to care about the small things. Numbers are what's important. I will tell you, so please tell the people. GNP per person grew from $319 to $1,640. The economy grew 11 percent per annum. Finally, the rocket of Korean Peninsula has taken off. Toward a new world called 'advanced nation'..., and in that new world, a new Korea will be born. A home for upright and bright people, the new Korea will be born.

"Chief Secretary! General Kim! What are you doing? You just passed the main gate of the Blue House! Where

are you trying to go? Chief Secretary! I'm begging you. Don't take me to the Army Hospital. You have to bury that body deep in the earth. No soul can dwell in that body."

At that moment, the CIA director is taking action to seize power. He goes to the Army Chief of Staff[13] who has been standing by at a safe house in Gungjeong-dong. He merely says, "The President has been in an accident," without revealing what really happened and recommends announcing martial law. At the Chief of Staff's suggestion, they ride a car together to go to the command center of the Army Headquarters at Namsan hill. The president's soul continues his monologue.

"I can see Namsan.[14] I can see a car going around the foot of Namsan and entering the Army Headquarter compound. I can see the CIA director and Chief of Staff in the back seat.

"Chief Jung! Look carefully at the foolishness of that man next to you. An old man's foolishness has a mysterious power, just as an old man's lust makes him

frivolous, to make him forget his place and susceptible to flattery and fall for the seductions of powerful men. That man has lost himself to the lure of cheese-stinking Iago's lies and doesn't even realize that a moment ago he strangled to death a life inside the womb, a life to be named "Nuclear" who would have brought his nation pride and revival.

"Chief Jung! Have you imagined our descendants who will play to the fiddle of fickle Americans? Have you pictured the image of our descendants who will be helpless before the tyranny of vicious Japanese? Our precious boy Nuclear who would have shown his face to the world in a year and half, that boy could have been Korea's Moses. As he liberated the oppressed Jews from Egypt, that boy would have liberated us from our disgraceful history. He would have freed us from the history of siding with either China or Japan, forced to pimp for them.

"Ah, now everything has been all in vain. Because the CIA director's foolishness led him to believe the sweet words of arrogant Americans or the vile Japanese who turned into Iago….

"Chief Jung! But don't blame them. You have to understand the Americans, why they have to listen to Japan to keep her as their ally after making them the only nation in human history to be victims of the nuclear bomb. And you only need to understand Japan's fear of the potential nuclear capability of her neighbor. We must have a strong friend far away, America to check a strong neighbor nearby, Japan. And we need a strong ally nearby, Japan to keep in check another strong neighbor, China. Two strong neighbors, Japan and China... we have to make these two huge locomotives take on the role of pushing and pulling the Korean Peninsula from front and back. Chief Jung! Please leave these words as my advice for the leaders of the next generation.

"Ah, the fog is pressing upon me. The fresh touch of the mist on my cheeks. I will sweep away the mist with my hands. The man in the black robe has come down the stairs and is taking long strides toward me. The old man's warm smile, more wise and affectionate than the smile of an old mother welcoming her son back safe from the battlefield. The kindness of his smile tells me

that whatever sin I committed in the world is forgiven. Finally, I think I feel a sense of peace in my heart. Everything I see is lovely. At last, I feel the confidence to love and cherish everything I touch. The old man is putting out his hand. I will hold his hand. Huh! Why is the woman doing that? The woman hiding behind the old man suddenly kneels in front of him. She is holding the hand he held out to me and desperately pleading with him…. Why? Ah, she is turning her face. Oh! It's Young-soo!

'Young-soo! Young-soo!'

"She is gesturing me to leave. Young-soo! I will never go back. Our children are young? It can't be helped. I will not go back. Please don't abandon me. Young-soo, I can't bear even you abandoning me. What saved me from the suffering that even death could not end was meeting you, a devil and an angel's meeting. Young-soo, our eyes did not meet on our first encounter. You chose me after seeing me just from the back. Watching my bent back while I was lacing my combat shoes, you thought I looked manly and trustworthy.

"Young-soo! Your innocence, your beautiful heart

became a warm sunlight and put to sleep the turbulent waves churning in the endless sea. You saved an old ship just before being wrecked. Your generosity, your patience, your beauty became a tender magnolia and transformed a raging devil into a poet. So I wrote poems of hope.

'All that I lack, all my flaws will be absorbed, embraced and settled by your vast womanly character, good and gentle. Then will be refined and perfected into a man's character.'

"This poem was a solemn vow I made to God, to live the remainder of my life as a humble man as a caring father and affectionate husband.

"Ah, but that vow was never something that I could keep. Because of the dream that filled my heart to the brim. That dream which began when I was a cadet of the Japanese Army Academy was to enable the motherland to escape forever from hunger by setting up the heavy and chemical industries. Because I knew the source of Japan's power lay in the modern factories

when I visited them as a cadet. That was a flame burning from a furnace and an endless maze of steel pipes.

"It wasn't something landowners' politician sons or prodigals could dare to attempt. They accepted the country's poverty as fate, and reigning over the farmers, they had never known hunger. But soldiers, we who were sons of farmers, felt poverty firsthand, in our bones. On top of that, we were unique in receiving modern education. We had a duty to modernize the nation. And sadly, I came to stand at the front of that lot.

"Ah, but it was not an easy thing! The viper of fatalism that had bedded the people over a thousand years would not leave their side. Every night, that viper would burrow itself into the people's bed, furtively lie down and sought to sleep with them. Then it would flick its tongue and run its mouth.

'You can't do it, you are a loser, you just have to accept being poor!'

"I realized then that the past is a tough thing that no present can ever erase. I realized the truth that the only way to hide the past is to create a future that is totally

different from the past.

"So I decided to create such a future. A future for farmers who won't know any barley humps,[15] *for farms without straw-thatched huts, for a country of wilderness turned into green fields, for a country's industry that can build ships and cars, for the Korean people who will no longer be scorned but respected.... I called all this national modernization, people's revitalization, economic independence, and self-reliant national defense, and I resolved to fight the viper head on.*

"I raised my body from the haven in which I hid with you, drew my sword, sang revolutionary songs, and called out the viper. The viper then shrank with fear and crawled into the ground.

"Young-soo! I conquered the viper. At least I prided myself thinking that I had conquered it. Ah, but it was too soon to be proud! The viper squirmed under the dirt and then slithered out again. It cried, 'Democracy' and burrowed into the heart of the masses and spawned treachery. I found out in the mud pit of so-called 'elections' that the innocent woman I loved was actually a whore. You will never understand how a man feels

when he is betrayed. A phantom that I can't persuade or grasp, wielding the power of numbers that I can't ignore, the masses were like a prostitute who knew no gratitude and was beset by forgetfulness.

"The prostitute ignored the rescuer who saved her from an obscene life called poverty, and then, spurred on by vile pimps, craving for a deeper orgasm called freedom, she was casting a wicked glance of seduction to a strong, young man who was shouting false 'freedom'.

"I began suffering from loneliness. Loneliness turned into boredom.... Do you know what a betrayed man wants when he is bored? War. I wanted a war. The sounds of cannons, jets, groans, stench of blood.... That moment when everything comes to a standstill prior to all these brings peace to the heart of a lonely and bored man.

"Yushin was the war I chose. I resolved to lead a great Yushin army to the battlefield and become a hero who defeats poverty and will forever be memorialized in the history of human warfare.

"I made everyone who noisily prattled on my enemies,

but I welcomed as my friends the masses who remained silent in the invisible shadows. I was listening to the sound of their hot, thunderous imaginary applause. On nights when sleep would not come, I tried to sleep to the sound of their clapping, and smiled as I drew their faces in my mind.

"I violently put to sleep the noisemakers. But I couldn't escape the look of their souls' eyes. Even now, their reproaching eyes have become razor sharp knives and they are plunging and digging into my heart. The reproachful look of someone who has spent his whole life in resentment, the blank stare of someone who has lost the desire to live at the violence of a compatriot, the terrified eyes of young people who are grinding their teeth at the humiliation suffered at the hands of fellow human beings in a dark basement, the screaming eyes of a mother who lost a son and is clawing her chest, those eyes…."

The mother's screaming eyes recede into the distance and turn into mothers wearing black mourning clothes. Their hairs disheveled, they raise high their fists and scream.

"Curse on you! The cruelest curse will fall on you! Your soul will fall in pain. Pain a thousand times worse than the pain I suffered.... Do you know what a mother feels, who longs to see her son through an endless night? Curse, curse, curse.... The cruelest curse will fall on your child."

The president yells at them.

"I fervently beg you..., please, at least leave my son alone!

"My son who couldn't be born to a common man.... My son who will be dreaming of his mother who was taken away by an assassin's bullet as he sleeps in a cold tent in the Military Academy, please just leave him alone. Instead, I will rip out the skin off my chest and throw myself at your knives of vengeance. Please, just leave my son alone!

"Young-soo! Where are you going? You are following them, they who are cursing our child? Please, don't go with them. Why are you trying to leave me? Please come and hold my hand. Please draw me to where you

are. Why are you trying to abandon me? What? What? What are you saying? Ah, I understand. I will do as you say. I will go back to earth and say my last words, and then I will follow you.

"My soul is slowly descending to earth. Into the body inside the car.

"Chief Secretary! Your arms are warm, and your knees soft. Stop your tears. I came back into my body to leave you my last words. Let go of the rage in your heart. Director Kim actually ended my suffering. Just existing in this world, that alone was excruciating suffering for me. I need to be freed from that pain. Chief Secretary! Please convey every single word I leave behind.

"History! Coldhearted and violent history! Take these last words as my final request. Don't treat too severely the ill-fated life of a pitiful dictator who made his beloved wife pour blood from her breast at an assassin's bullet, then lived in loneliness, and now must die at a killer's bullet and leave behind a young son. What I want now is oblivion, from my people, nation, my nation's mountains and fields, and my nation's history.

Just remember me as a pitiful man who begs and pleads for his beloved history not to hate him, even after it has abandoned him.

"You politicians! You who gather your minions to build a marketplace to wheedle the sweat-stained money out of the hands of naïve and goodhearted citizens with your false call for democracy! Receive solemnly these words as my last warning. I won't say anything about your gambling den in which you tear at each other. But don't drag the innocent into that den and corrupt them. If you keep just that promise, I will look away. But please don't gamble with the people's future and the people's suffering. Whatever flowery words flow from your lips like a sleek river, whatever unfathomable performance you put on, the treacherous intentions hidden in your heart will one day be revealed. Have you tried to remember the young daughters of our people who forgot all sense of shame and threw off their clothes before foreigners solely because of hunger?

"Did you ever stop to think, just once, of our people's sons who had to stretch out their hands, begging for cookie crumbs from gangly yankees? History is a fickle

thing. If history turns crazy again and doesn't punish you, the sorrowful sighs of fathers and mothers will become a tornado that overturns the great earth and throw you politicians' filthy bodies out of this world.

"My good people! Please take these words as my farewell. No matter what anyone suffered because of me, please remember the pitiful passing of a lonely ruler who is dying in pain. If that is not enough, I will gladly take whatever suffering you give me even in the afterlife. And far in the future, if I have the joy of looking down and seeing Korea become an Asian superpower, I will turn over to you all that joy.

"My daughters![16] *You were always so good! How can I express the sorrow of a father who must leave after hurling you to this brutal world. Scold this useless father all you want. Ah, my heart is tearing apart, I want to be punished by this pain forever. You who are incomparably more precious than my life or any worldly honor, you who loved your father more than any other children in the world. Your father who has made you into forsaken orphans, the only thing he can say is sorry. But forget your worthless father and be strong*

and live fully. If there is an afterlife—there must be—I promise I will wait for you there. And there, I will spend the days, wearing a straw hat, with rolled up sleeves and trouser legs, tending the fields and tilling the soil, whiling away the evening preparing cowfeed, and the night, sitting by your mother twisting straw ropes.

"Son! Although you were not beside me, your existence gave fearless strength and drive to me. You were always in my mind and moved me with your dignified, soundless voice. For the future of the country where you will live, I would exchange my life for a handful of dirt without hesitation, and to leave you an inheritance of honor, I was prepared to accept any severe suffering, any violence that would enrage the world, and any cowardly deceit.

"Ah, this small heart is being ripped into a hundred thousand pieces and all the blood in my body is surging up my throat! If I could only write on the barren earth with this blood from my mouth, forgive me, your worthless father!

"My poor son! No matter how fickle and violent history is, no one can deny this one truth. The truth that

I made the stripped mountains of our country green again, that I drove out the thatched root huts from our farmlands, that I forever eliminated spring hunger from our country's farmers…. When the time comes, even if no one can tell when, someone will understand that my stubbornness, my tenacity, and my violence was the fount of abundance. When that time comes, my son, you will remember as a happy memory all that you suffered as an orphan who lost his father and mother to an assassin's bullet. My poor son! Receive these as my last words. That your father who loved you more than anyone begs for your forgiveness.

"General Kim! For a man who used his silence as a shield, I think I've prattled on too much. The tongue always brings harm! Now send me to Young-soo. If time still remains, then turn back the seasons and take me to Moraesil[17] *where I spent my childhood. I want to see last my home where I grew up.*

"Spring in Moraesil always started at the back of the village, on the lawn of the cemetery next to the ancestral shrine. I can see clearly a young boy shooting bamboo arrows and playing soldier among the neighborhood

kids on the grassy field, softened as the warm sunlight thaws the ground. By the time the dark draws near and he is covered with sweat, the boy runs back home with his hands clasping his hungry stomach. When he sits to eat a bowl of rice and vegetable porridge his mother puts before him, it always tastes as good as honey.

"Summer in Moraesil always infused the young boys of the village with vigor. Watching in the distance the old men and women sitting on straw mats and playing jangi[18] *under the elm tree, summer meant freedom from the stern gaze of adults for the young boys, splashing about naked in the streams.*

"Autumn in Moraesil brought the boys colorful clothes and food. Having wandered single file with wooden rifles on the shoulders between the fields covered with ears of rice, the boy would come home as the sun set. When his mother would greet him with a happy smile unexplainable to him, he would feel the impulse to start whining.

"Winter in Moraesil never failed to find us when we would start feeling the itch to zoom our sleds across the frozen rice paddies. To the young boys of Moraesil,

winter meant beef soup and white rice. One New Year's Day, I can see a boy dressed in colorful clothes and kicking a jegi[19] *in an alley after filling himself up with beef soup and white rice.*

"Ah, I miss the poor life in Moraesil. Its poverty did not leave anybody lonely."

The car carrying the President and the Chief Secretary arrives at the gate of the Armed Forces Capital Hospital.

"Stop!"

The guard shouts and blocks the road. The Chief Secretary rolls down the window.

"It's me, Presidential Chief Secretary. Let us in quickly!"

The guard salutes at the Chief Secretary's shout.

"Yes sir! Proceed."

The Chief Secretary looks at his wristwatch. It is pointing exactly at 7:55 pm. It is the moment when the president breathes his last breath. It has been exactly 15 minutes since the bullet fired by the CIA director pierced the president's chest.

Appendix 2

President Park Chung-hee, His Dedication and Legacy

(Collection of articles serialized in *The Chosun Ilbo*[1] during the funeral in 1979)

Translated by Won-Jae Hur

1 Agricultural Modernization

<The New Community Movement>[2] "Escaping 5,000 Years of Poverty"

Income Increase Achieved through Nurturing Independence

1969 when the drive to increase farming and fishing income was moving ahead full steam. At the former citizen's hall in Saejongno, an evaluation competition of the farming fishing income project had opened. Included in the program was the then-still-novel session called, "My Success Story Presentation." Mr. Ha Sa-yong from Jochiwon was the presenter.

Mr. Ha, who had worked as a farmhand, became married but had no way to make a living. He made a promise with his recently married wife, "I will go to Gangwon-do[3] and work three more years as a farmhand, can you work as a maid during that time? Three years later, let's meet back in Jochiwon and use the money to make it on our own." The couple stayed true to their promise.

Three years later, Mr. and Mrs. Ha met again as they had pledged, lived in a dugout in place of a house, and started farming in a plastic greenhouse by a riverbed. Things seemed to be going well when Mr. Ha fell ill from a pulmonary disease due to excessive strain. They had to spend all their savings on medical care. Even though he had to battle the illness, he did not despair but fought on. As time passed, he recovered his health, gained financial stability, and even acquired a house with a new slate roof, a rarity at the time.

The person who was filled with more excitement and emotion than anyone else as people listened to this success story was President Park Chung-hee. President Park put aside his prepared speech and launched into an impromptu speech. He emphasized, "Mr. Ha is the kind of leader and mentor who will lead the farms, and we must learn from such a leader." Several months later, when the Monthly Economic Trends Report Conference was finished, President Park said, "The statistical numbers are fine, but it will be good to listen to success stories of farmers and fishermen who are working to make a good living as well as the research reports on economic trends by academics." Thus began the two-person Saemaul Success Story Presentations at the time of the Monthly Economic Trends Report Conference.

As the Monthly Economic Report Conference usually gathers together former government ministers, ruling party ministers, Presidential Secretary, and ministers of the Office of Prime Minister, it points out in timely fashion key obstacles and issues in newly developing the agricultural sector. A barrage of issues pours forth, such as riverway repairs, village improvement, electricity, water systems, roads, and others that the government needs to support or farmers and fishermen need to address on their own. President Park records in memo all the essential items. For three years, until the end of 1971 when the New Community Movement was actually implemented, President Park's cherished intention to address the future and problems of agriculture was concretely fulfilled.

President Park showed his interest in agriculture in his policy soon after he took power in 1961. Whenever he saw a farm during his visits to the provinces, he would be in pain and say, "I can't forget that seeping out of that warped straw-roofed house are the sighs of farmers steeped in thousand years of poverty." Then he would tell stories of how his deceased father lived a hard life growing rice on half an acre of land, and how he made a ball out of wood and twine because he wanted to play soccer but couldn't afford a ball.

When he received reports of farms suffering from usurious loans, he resolved to end such loans and began the national reconstruction movement.

The national reconstruction movement, however, did not go as he desired. It was said that people did not promote it because they concluded that the farms were so poor that they did not have the capacity to get back to their feet on their own. Furthermore, at the time, the administration did not have the surplus to pour resources into the farms and fisheries.

Building up the resources, the period between

1967-68 can be seen as the time when President Park drove forward the modernization of agriculture. After the completion of phase 1 and phase 2 of the Five-Year Economic Development Plan, the government's financial capability greatly improved due to the export-led growth and industrialization policies. It became possible at this time to take up again the challenge of agricultural modernization. During this period, compared to the 5% income tax, the government support to the agricultural sector was at 26%. The dynamic of modernization had begun to penetrate into the agricultural sector from the outside. Sericulture industry, special crops industry, and other staple products industries were created so that the phrase "income increase" became commonly used, and land development began to take shape. President Park would visit the farming regions several times every month. During the Yeongsan River development in South Cholla Province, he personally drafted the illustrations that would serve as the basis for development, and made eight trips to this site alone over two years. In 1968, for the first time the agricultural special income project was listed as a line item in the budget.

After the government's economic capability increased, and President Park acquired a realistic and detailed grasp of the problems in the agricultural sector through the Success Story Presentations, he appears to have been searching for an opportunity to set fire to the agricultural modernization movement in the 1970s.

In the spring of 1971, Ssangyong corporation completed the factory for mass cement production. The factory output far exceeded domestic demand. The government bought the cement at low prices and allotted five sacks per household in 35,000 villages across the country.

The condition was to prioritize using it for joint village enterprises. Several months later, the administration assessed the results of the cement use and found diverse results. Some villages made many-fold returns using the cement, while others had to "spend" it out of necessity. The records show approximately 16,000 villages making good returns. The successful villages had in common a mentality of active participation by residents and a leader who fully embodied it. On this basis, villages across the country were categorized as beginner village, self-helping village, and independent village.

Industriousness - Self-Reliance - Cooperation Consciousness Revolution, Number One Priority for National Policy

The mentality of industriousness, self-reliance, and cooperation was also emphasized. At the end of 1971, all these factors came together to ignite the modernization effort called the New Community Movement. In reality, the actual implementation preceded the naming of the New Community Movement.

Park Jin-hwan, Special Assistant to the President, recollected that President Park, seeing the New Community Movement successfully promoted, made the assessment, "The plan to raise up a movement to awaken an attitude of self-reliance in the people and the desire to live well finally succeeded on the third try."

Park regrets deeply the fact that he did not ask the

President then what first and second attempts he had in mind, thinking "I have to ask him about the history behind the New Community Movement when the time comes," and never getting that chance. He said that the first attempt was certainly the national reconstruction movement, but the second attempt is unclear. Perhaps, he surmises, it was the second economic development movement.

President Park stipulated that the New Community Movement was the true legacy and advancement of the May 16th Revolution philosophy, and shows our people, filled with hope and desire, sprinting to complete fully our nation's modernization(May 16, 1972 Commemoration Speech)." He also stressed that we must "make the New Community Movement the number one task in national policy, foster through this movement a social character that voluntarily rectifies social improprieties, and implement a decisive policy of equal welfare (October 17, 1972 Announcement)."

President Park conducted the Movement simultaneously as a modernization policy and as an economic policy instrument for building a clean society without improprieties. Consequently, President Park's level of interest in New Community leadership contest and New Community training center was astounding. The President himself dropped in without warning at the New Community training center in Suwon, listening for an hour to a lecture in the back seat, or they would eat noodle lunches with trainees and discuss their thoughts about the New Community Movement. The fact that desks were placed in multileveled lecture halls so that people seated in the back could clearly see the lecturer's face and expressions, the installation of high-quality mikes, the detailed attention trainers paid when asking about the content of the answers written by the trainees to their questions, all of these things reflected how great was President Park's interest in the Movement.

Special Emphasis on "My Ancestor is a 'New Community Farmer'"

President Park thought of his time spent with New Community leaders as one of the most enjoyable part of his strenuous work schedule. Whenever he had a luncheon with them, he frequently asked the covering reporters, "Please introduce with good words these people who have overcome adversities to improve the farms." Rather than reading a speech prepared by the secretary office, he often gave impromptu talks at meetings with New Community leaders. Although he spoke more plainly than what was in the written speech, the participants responded with great enthusiasm. This was possible because he was the son of a farmer and intimately knew farmers. As we can see from his statement at the New Community leader contest on November 22, 1973, "When in the future someone asks who were your ancestors, let people say my ancestor was a leading farmer in the New Community Movement in the 1970s," he considered the Movement leadership as important as any national leader.

In President Park's promotion of agricultural modernization through the New Community Movement, he considered important a revolution in consciousness through self-awareness. "Rural modernization can never be accomplished by simply looking at the sky waiting for good fortune or impatiently expecting immediate results. Having no harvest in autumn without planting seeds in spring, that is farming. Only with the will for independence which strives to improve one's destiny by oneself before desiring another's help, and which takes responsibility before blaming others, can individuals live well and the nation rise up." President Park would emphasize this point whenever he had the opportunity. He also frequently quoted the proverb, "God helps those who help themselves." Not only did he emphasize and quote these words, he also acted on them.

President Park chose to give government support first to independent villages in the country that clearly demonstrated the will and effort to improve their lives. He sought to provoke the sense of independence in farmers by fomenting competition through benefits such as free provisions for bridge construction, deployment of engineers, and priority in electricity supply. An independent village would have a signpost installed at the entrance that said, "Independent Village," thereby raising the pride of its residents. Struggling 'beginner villages' that began with the same conditions but watched their neighboring town transform showed, as expected, a strong competitive spirit. One beginner village of fifty or so households held a village council and voluntarily demolished 10 houses in order to revamp the village. Saving campaigns led by economizing-rice campaign leaders, mother's associations, and other associations spread like wildfire. The people began having the confidence that they could do it if they tried.

What President Park sought to build on top of this kind of mental awareness was the income expansion project. He judged that no matter how good the New Community Movement was, if the farmers did not see concrete benefits such as income increase, the movement would have no permanence. However, while connecting this income expansion project with the New Community Movement was correct in principle, it was a risky decision in terms of maintaining a leader's popularity. Since income increase is something that must happen in fact, should the increase to which the farmers assented fail to materialize, all the effort spent on promoting the New Community Movement and modernization would result in failure. President Park, however, did not linger on such worries expressed around him and began a bold income expansion project. This also became the occasion for moving into the second phase of the agricultural modernization.

On December of 1972, Kim Bo-hyun, Minister of Agriculture and Fisheries, received a thick handwritten letter from President Park. When he opened it, he was stunned. Six pages of white lined paper were filled with notes of the President's plans and thoughts for food increase, self-support, and self-sufficiency. *Tongil*(unification) rice[4] supply, high rice purchase price policy, insulated rice seed bed, the process from planting to threshing, 150 days of events and reforms were all written down in detail, said Minister Kim. At the tasting party after the Ministry of Agriculture and Fisheries finished the experimental cultivation of *Tongil* rice(called IR667), President Park expressed his satisfaction saying, "We can now say farewell to the 'barley hump'." Then the President proceeded to tell the story of how he packed only barley rice for lunch when he was a child.

There are probably very few people who will object when it is said that the fact our farms can now enjoy cultural benefits such as TVs, refrigerators, and talk of automated farming are all fruition of President Park's dedication to income expansion. It may be that after World War II, among so many countries, none except for ours and Taiwan have attracted attention because they have transformed agriculture as quickly as we have.

<*The Chosun Ilbo,* October 31, 1979>

We Must Run while Others Rest.

Income Increase Monthly Inspection - Encouragement

From 1962 to last September, there is one council that President Park has presided over and never missed even once. That is the Council for Expansion of Export Promotion.

This council, which changed its name to Trade Promotion Council two years ago, is attended by the Prime Minister, Chairman of the Board of Audit and Inspection, ministers of relevant ministries, leading ruling party members, policy consultation personnel, heads of the four economic divisions, and around 200 representatives of export businesses.

In the council meeting, the relevant authorities of the

Ministry of Foreign Affairs first reports on problems related to export commodities recorded by embassies abroad and strategy. Then, the commerce division offers evaluation and recommendations on measures addressing the previous month's actual export results and variation ratio of the previous month's expenditures. Afterward, the business representatives disclose current difficulties and the relevant ministers give their input.

After listening to the views of business representatives and relevant authorities, whose positions are different, President Park makes a synthesized prescription. Getting the right price, raising product quality, and other series of export strategies were created through such a process.

The President formed this council with the adoption of the 'Export First' principle. Around 1963, pre- and post-election, our foreign currency holdings fell under 100 million US dollars and we were heading toward bankruptcy, so that even though we had factories, it was difficult to operate them. In this situation, President Park concluded that the only way our economy could survive was through exports, and ran this council as part of formulating the policy of 'Export Nation'. Accordingly, the truth is that President Park poured more of his passion into this council than any other council.

Since 2 to 3 years ago, there has been talk in the commerce division of holding this council every other month, or even every quarter. They opined whether it was necessary to meet every month when export expansion was going smoothly and showing no particular problems. There also seems to have been an ulterior motive to decrease the toil involved in preparing for the council meetings.

Every time, however, President Park urged them more strenuously. He would command, "If we are to advance in every area, we must run faster when others are running fast, and we must continue running when others are resting. Only then can there be advancement."

Forbidding his subordinates to grow slack, his stubbornness and dedication to presiding over the council every month finally led to the rapid increase of exports in just thirteen years, from 100 million US dollars in 1964 to 10 billion US dollars by 1977, and made the council into the 'miracle maternity ward'.

When we look at the statistics of the world's nations, 10% growth per annum in exports is considered to be quite high. If we take 42,900,000 dollars in 1961 as the base and make a calculation with 20% annual increase in exports, that still reaches only 1 billion 142,000,000 dollars in 1979. When we consider from this perspective that the country reached 12.5 billion dollars last year alone, and set this year's goal as 15.5 billion dollars, we can begin to appreciate truly the immense magnitude of our export growth.

It was decisively due to President Park's blazing conviction that we must achieve 'Export Nation'. Knowing no compromise, President Park's dedication to national modernization also clearly manifested during the construction of the Gyeongbu Expressway.

Gyeongbu Highway Construction, Opportunity for Exporting Technology, Nurturing Confidence and Heading toward Age of Heavy and Chemical Industries

When President Park set his sights on constructing the Gyeongbu Highway[5] in the latter half of the 1960s, many in the domestic economic, academic, and media sectors opposed it outright. Even ruling party members countered that it was impossible to achieve, and that it will bring economic ruin. The World Bank and international nongovernmental economic organizations also shared the same opinion.

President Park, however, without a hint of wavering, received and meticulously scrutinized reports from domestic consultants. He ordered his assistants to collect and bring to him every record they could find on highway construction from around the world, from the Andes Mountains in South America to the plains of Russian Siberia, and he personally examined the collected documents. He spent many weekends riding the helicopter with the construction division engineers, inspecting the topography of the included areas. It is said that during this time, even the corridors and the cafeteria of the Blue House, not to mention every office, were covered with maps, diagrams, and other materials on the highway construction.

Gaining his confidence, President Park finally pushed the start button for construction in the Seoul-Suwon corridor on February 1, 1968. At the time, even as they acknowledged that this construction was a historical project, every news outlet expressed grave concern over economic stability due to loans for raising 40 billion won in construction costs and other issues. They also regarded with suspicion the prospect that it would proceed as planned. Even the ground-breaking ceremony received a cold reception, garnering only small attention in the papers.

Confirming on Site from Planning to Completion

While the construction proceeded, President Park went back and forth countless times to the construction site by helicopter. When the base of a mountain collapsed during tunnel construction, he brought geological experts and inquired about the cause, and called in the UN water systems expert to find out how the calculations for the underground waterway went wrong.

Two years and 25 months later, on June 30, 1970, the 428 km four-lane Gyeongbu Highway was almost miraculously completed. Transportation experts at the Asia Development Bank gaped at the fact that the construction costs per 1 km came out to 330,000 US dollars (then 100 million won), the cheapest in world highway construction history. ECAPE (Economic Commission for Asia and the Far East) experts on the roads committee stated after the test drive that there were no defects in their assessment.

In just three years after the Gyeongbu Highway opened, the region that utilized the highway produced nearly 30% of our nation's GNP, and the number of vehicles using the highway took up more than 80% of the nation's total number of vehicles.

It cannot be denied that this too is the outcome of President Park's dedication and foresight. The method of highway construction planning and design acquired through the Gyeongbu Highway construction process, the standardization of materials, establishment of the system of mass production all became the decisive foundation for the Korean construction industry's future overseas expansion. It is the matrix for the Korean construction technology that is renowned in the South Asia-Middle East region, and it became the source of foreign currency earnings.

In his book *The People's Potential*, he wrote, "The successful construction of Gyeongbu Highway, which was the greatest building project in our people's history, proves our people's superb potential and powerful resolve. It was a project that carries the significance of awakening pride and confidence in our ability to accomplish whatever we set out to do."

President Park's dedication came from the desire that "We too should live well," the conviction that "We also can live well," and the determination that, "We must become an independent, self-supporting people who can live by our own strength without another's help, and even have the capacity to help others." Behind this conviction is President Park's experience of growing up in a poor farming family and living in a poor country half his life, which was sublimated into an almost fiery and indomitable competitive spirit.

In December 1964, President Park and First Lady Yuk

Young-Soo made a state visit to West Germany.[6] When President Park saw the rich West German countryside, he said with envy, "When will there be electricity and water in farms, and when will we be rid of thatch roof shacks in our country?" Beside the countryside, it is said that when he compared the West German progress with our economic situation, ours was so pitiful and miserable that he felt almost embarrassed.

The story goes that as he was riding in a leased airplane on his way back from West Germany, he said, "Until our per capita income exceeds $1,000 and we can fly our own airplane, let's not go on foreign visits."

It was around this time that the project to transform agriculture and fisheries began in earnest, and the farming village assistance project spread like wildfire from 1978.

The commitment to national modernization and independent economy went from 'Export as Number One Priority' to 'Industrialized Nation' and 'Science Nation, Independent Technology', and laid the foundation to become a leading Asian industrialized nation after Japan.

As President Park declared, "As the Aswan High Dam is the symbol of the Nasser Revolution, the Uljin Industrial Complex and the 5-Year Economic Development Plan Phase 1 can be considered as the symbols of the May 16 Revolution," the 5-Year Economic Development Plan Phase 1 embodied the will to industrialize.

During this period, the emphasis was on preparing the necessary foundations for industrialization, such as electric power, coal, and other energy resources and cement, fertilizer, refined oil, and synthetic resins. As a result, we achieved an average annual economic growth of 7.8% and 250 million US dollars in exports in 1966, a six-fold increase from 1961.

During Phase 2, various structural foundations and development plans were put in place. as part of a three-pronged strategic project for growing the petrochemistry, steel, and machinery industries. With the Ulsan Petrochemistry Complex built in 1967, Honam Oil completed in 1969, and Pohang Iron and Steel Company beginning construction in 1970, the curtain rose on the heavy and chemical industrial age in the 1970s.

When Pohang Iron and Steel was completed in 1973 and phase 1 of the Hyundai Shipyard finished in 1974, two ships weighing 260,000 tons were launched. Each time such important projects began and finished, President Park would personally visit the site to encourage the participants, demonstrating the great strength of his dedication to national modernization.

President Park judged that the most important resource for our economic development were the people's energy, creativity, perseverance, and willpower. He, therefore, thought that his chief duty was to inspire confidence and courage so that the people would wholeheartedly unite and commit to achieving the goals of modernization and economic independence. Whenever someone created a new product or performed well at the Worldskills Competition, he would invite the person to the Blue House, encourage them, and raise their courage.

This year, with the completion of the copper refinery and Yeochun Petrochemicals, the heavy and chemical industrialization plan has been successfully realized. It is said that President Park had mapped out the concrete program for an ambitious industrial policy for the upcoming 1980s and planned to announce it at the end of this year or the beginning of next year.

Yet, more than the material constructions such as factories and roads or statistical numbers, what is truly compelling about the foundation for economic independence established under President Park can be felt personally by each citizen. The term 'barley hump' has disappeared from our midst, and our ears have become accustomed to the words 'middle class'.

What is more precious than this is that the self-disparaging sense of inferiority has disappeared from our people's consciousness. 'We can do it', 'We'll give a go', 'We also can become an advanced nation', people have come to possess this kind of positive attitude. We can say that President Park's commitment to economic independence has awakened the people's will and confidence, and it has allowed them to rediscover their dignity and pride.

In his book *Our Nation's Path*, President Park declared that the important goal of people's prosperity and happiness lies in "the guarantee of the individual's economic life," and "The first task that we must accomplish is building an independent economy and instilling in the people confidence in their own capability."

Also, on the first-floor wall of the Government Building, President Park's words are engraved on a marble plaque:

"When our descendants ask us who are living today what we did for them and for the nation, let us live so that we can say with a clear conscience and without hesitation that we worked and worked with an unfailing faith in national modernization."

The quote comes from the President's State of the Nation address given on January 17, 1967.

Despite President Park Chung-hee's untimely death, he will be judged as having fulfilled at least his two dreams that he held up like religious faith. How we will strengthen the basis of national modernization and economic independence that he established and make them flourish is the work for those of us who remain.

<*The Chosun Ilbo,* November 1, 1979>

Our Predecessor's Legacy is the Site of Patriotic Education

Nurturing Traditional Culture within Mindset of Self-Reliance

One Monday morning in June of 1977, Minister Kim Sung-jin of the Ministry of Culture received a call from the Blue House saying, "Come quickly," and hurriedly left. Having prepared a minibus, President Park, his son Ji-man, and several security officers were waiting. When he arrived, he promptly drove the car to Ganghwa Island. Visiting by turn historical sites where we fought Mongols during the Goryeo period and other foreign countries, he ordered repairs and restorations for the Gwanghwa Island sites.

At the site of the Gwanghwa Island Treaty, when Minister Kim asked, "Is it really necessary to restore this place that is connected to a humiliating history?" President Park said, "That's not how it is. Since our ancestors suffered such insult by their mistakes, we must restore this place so that we can mark well here the import of never repeating such a history of humiliation." After carefully examining the General Eo Jae-yeon[7] Pavillion, he said, "When commemorating history, we have to record not only the general's achievements but, in a fair manner, also record and praise the nameless soldiers who sacrificed their lives under him." He then ordered that a monument be built for the nameless soldiers below the Pavillion. Subsequently, a memorial tablet or monument for nameless soldiers was always constructed as part of the restoration of other sites, such as the 700 Righteous Warriors and ancestral shrines of historical militia leaders.

President Park always said that national defense heritage sites where our ancestral martyrs overcame endless foreign invasions and all manner of hardships are the truly precious national cultural inheritance, and that they were the sites for social education that nurtures love for country and patriotism in the people. Accordingly, President Park gave a lot of his energy to reviving traditional culture and cleaning up and restoring national defense heritage sites of our ancestors, so that they could become the center point of our national awareness.

One day in the autumn of 1976, President Park without prior notice took along some government officials, looked around Yeoju where King Sejong's[8] royal tomb Yeongneung is located, and ordered that the dilapidated tomb be consecrated. When the Yeongneung consecration was finished after two years of construction, President Park was overjoyed as he rode in the car back to Seoul after the completion ceremony.

After Complaint that "The President Cares only about Military Affairs," "I Kept My Promise" on Sejong Royal Tomb Consecration

"I kept my promise," he said. When someone sitting

by him asked what promise, President Park confided, "When I expanded and consecrated Chungmugong's Hyeonchungsa,[9] I heard that many people in the academy and cultural world complained, 'The President only cares about generals because he himself came from the military.' I couldn't answer every complaint, so I made a promise to myself. It wasn't that I cared only about generals, I simply set the priority straight. So I promised that I will build up a historical site of someone who had left behind a great legacy in culture, arts, and scholarship, as well as I did for Hyeonchungsa."

President Park judged that among King Sejong's accomplishments, the invention of the Korean script was a modern Korean cultural revolution, an expression of self-reliant consciousness, and a remarkable innovation (President Park's *Our Nation's Path*). He therefore took the decisive step of using Korean in all government documents. President Park repeatedly said that among the many valuable cultural inheritances, the major watershed moment for Korean culture was the Korean script, and every time he faced a difficulty, he would think about King Sejong who created the Korean script in face of the nobility's opposition.

When people were moving cultural artifacts for the '5000 Years of Korean Art Exhibit' in Japan, President Park would order, "Don't think of those cultural artifacts as just artifacts. Think of them as the spirit of our ancestors traveling to Japan for a short visit, and give your wholehearted effort to their preservation." He expressed a greater love for traditional culture than anyone else. Underneath President Park's attitude to traditional culture lay a deeply held attitude of self-reliance, and we can say that his self-reliant national defense, independent economy, pro-nation education, and a variety of policies supporting the people's revival emerged from it.

As expressions of this attitude of self-reliance, Korean studies and classics translation, repair and restoration of various cultural assets such as Heyeonchungsa, Ojukheon, and other sites, creating an education charter, and other projects that would typically take a long time were completed in 10 years or are in the process of being completed.

In early January of last year, President Park visited

the construction site for the Academy of Korean Studies at the foot of Guksa Peak of Cheonggye Mountain, despite suffering from a severe cold and the doctor's strict orders not to go out in the cold wind.

When Minister Kim returned after attending the 70-year commemoration of immigration to Hawaii and told President Park, "Old grandmothers and grandfathers who first immigrated to Hawaii have not forgotten our language and still wore our traditional clothes," the President ignored objections around him, drove straight to the Academy of Korean Studies construction site, and encouraged the construction personnel. Having personally chosen the site, which was renowned as an excellent piece of land, and toured the grounds, President Park said, "Please quickly start researching, formulate it in modern terms, and teach the young people what are traditional Korean thought and philosophy." This showed his passion for young people's cultural education.

As for the consecration of Hyeonchungsa, over two phases of construction between 1971-1974 the President Park personally went down countless times, and he knew the site down to its minute details, so that he could tell what was in what corner, and what variety of tree stood there, as if he were submitting a report to one of his assistants. President Park read books on history every chance he had. He acquired such thorough knowledge of modern history that he neared being an expert and made his associates flustered. His associates say that in the area of Chungmugong, the paragon of a soldier, he had reached the level of an expert scholar. President Park expressed detailed interest in any cultural asset restoration site, ranging from the traditional paintwork and lines to the variety of trees, and made a special effort to ask that the post-completion management be carried out thoroughly.

There were many repair and restorations of heritage sites including Chungiksa in Uiryong (General Gwak Jae-woo's shrine), Pyochungsa in Haenam (Seosan Daesa's shrine), Chungnyeolsa in Chungju (General Im Kyoung-eop's shrine), but with President Park's order in 1978 during the clean-up project of Goryeo Gungji on Gwanghwa Island, new standardized roof tiles that had better strength and shape than conventional tiles were issued.

President Park did not stop at conservation of national culture, but also exerted his effort into developing traditional culture in a rational manner. For example, there is the revamping of the Confucian model of life, which was formalistic and led to the vicious cycle of poverty, into the Simplified Family Rite Standards on March 5, 1969, and the Loyalty-Filial Piety-Courtesy model of life.

In the case of the latter, the effort to reestablish Eastern philosophy in a modern way generally received positive response, even though some academics opposed it saying, "It cannot be gain currency in a democratic society."

Among President Park's accomplishments, things like economic development can be seen in two to three years, but the fruit of what he did in scholarship, culture, and the arts will only become visible in 20 to 30 years. President Park promoted modernization, and to continue further his intentions in the cultural sphere, we must revive our cultural traditions, make them the basis for perpetually burning the flame of self-reliance in the people's hearts, said Minister of Culture Kim Sung-jin.

"A People of Advanced Technology, World Rule"... Founding of KIST

An area where President Park showed devotion almost equal to economic development, especially highway construction, was advancement in science and technology. During the early period of the revolution, he spent a great amount of effort in recruiting scientists through his teacher's training school classmate Kim Byung-hee(later President of Inha University School of Engineering), Atomic Research Institute director Choi Hyung-sup, and Kim Ki-young who had seven international patents in the ceramic industry. At last, he decided to invite topnotch Korean minds from abroad rather than domestic scientists, and after three years of labor, he made the decision to establish the Korea Institute of Science and Technology(KIST) as a gift for US President Lyndon Johnson's visit in 1966.

March of 1966, construction began with the ground-breaking ceremony in Hongneung, but the civilian-led construction work was sluggish. President Park occasionally would order Park Myung-geun(current Democratic Republican Party National Assemblymen), his assistant responsible for construction matters, "Prepare the car," go down to the construction site, and tried to encourage them to go forward. When, however, they made slow progress, he appointed a Colonel Choi as the head, organized a 'Construction Supervisory' consisting of graduated officers of the Military Academy who were experts in electricity, civil engineering, and architecture, and gave the fiery order, "Take responsibility for the construction and complete it quickly." KIST was built by these men in the end. At the beginning of the work, government officials overseeing cultural property preservation fiercely opposed the site selection, as if they had no clear understanding of the purpose of this institute.

In 1968 at the beginning-of-the-year press conference, President Park strongly stressed the need for developing science and technology saying, "The late 20th century will be ruled by people with advanced science and technology." President Park's plan to recruit talents abroad initially did not draw many volunteers and faced many difficulties. By various means such as annually hosting in Korea a conference of scientists working internationally, giving them a tour of the actual state of domestic economic development, and convincing them to return, KIST gradually took shape. Scientists who returned during the early period are now heads of various professional research institutes. When President Park received report that a large number of scientists who were to attend the conference had yet to fulfill their military service obligations and therefore faced difficulty travelling in and out of the country under current law, he decided to make an exception for attendees from 1973 on, despite the opposition of the Department of Defense.

As KIST took on a central role in national technology, President Park established a science school to train scientists in 1973. Seoul National University and others in the academia, however, fiercely opposed it saying, "Why make a science school when there are already masters programs in universities."

President Park pushed forward with the plan to establish the school when there were only a few supporters. As soon as the plan was decided, the Ministry of Education and Ministry of Science and Technology had a major confrontation over jurisdiction. Preparation for building alone took one and a half years due to matters such as creating new regulations for the science school, and the construction of the school buildings and facilities had to be done on credit as the costs were to be appropriated from the following year's budget.

After President Park's method of preferential treatment to scientists became widely known abroad, Dr. Lee Tae-gyu, once a nobel prize candidate, returned to become a professor at the science school in 1976. Hearing this news, President Park was overjoyed like a child. President Park sent his assistants to find out the scientists' salaries, housing situation, and other hospitality issues, and to inquire if there was anything they needed. The scientists were moved by the exceptional solicitude. From the beginning, President Park strongly emphasized the need to work hard in promoting science and technology and developing skilled technical manpower in order to sustain high rate of growth. He demonstrated especial interest in raising up technicians.

Just before Christmas in 1965, when First Lady Yuk was alive, President Park suddenly ordered his assistants, “Prepare 130 pounds of beef,” catching him off guard. His secretarial office had to go the US military base supply store in Samgakji and hastily prepare it, because at that time, regular butcheries did not have the facilities to store such a large amount of beef. Several hours later, President Park took the beef, went to the basic materials vocational training center in Bupyeong, and encouraged the technicians. Subsequently, the number of technical high schools that met international standards increased to 91, including Seongdong, Geumo, Busan technical high schools, and full-fledged establishment of technical training centers for each industry began. Furthermore, specialized colleges were designated in regional universities, and training talent in the sciences took off.

President Park strongly emphasized that we could

not expect to raise up heavy and chemical industries without technological development, and civilian corporations should not just expect government protection and support but must beat international competition through corporate streamlining and technological innovation. He also actively recommended installing technician training centers and research institutes in civilian companies. As a result, when for the first time Korea beat West Germany, Japan, and others to take combined first place at the 23rd Worldskills Competition in the Netherlands in 1977, President Park expressed great praise saying, “This is more wonderful and admirable than winning in any other field in an international contest.”

Our technological standard consists in KIST and approximately 20 specially designated professional research organizations in the 1960s. The distinguishing features of the 1970s comprised Gumi, Changwon, Yeocheon industrial complexes. Now in the civilian-led 1980s, we have before us building a science movement in the entire citizenry. President Park’s dedication to upholding traditional culture and raising up heavy and chemical industries is already entering a mature stage, but this inheritance must be continued until it blossoms and bears fruit.

<*The Chosun Ilbo,* November 2, 1979>

4 Independent National Defense

'Readiness is All', "I Myself Will Defend My Land"

Preparation for Withdrawal of Troops, Actualizing the Resolve for Self-Defense

We can see President Park Chung-hee's dedication to independent national defense in the fact that 30% of his discussions with foreign visitors was related to the subject. President Park always insisted that since our country is living under the threat of the North Korean puppet regime, the best protection of human rights was protecting the survival of 37 million people. Therefore, he pushed for making national security the first priority above all else, and promoted as his catchphrase "national development on one side and national defense on the other" under the call for "Defending My Own Land."

Since, however, the economic foundation was too weak to achieve independent national defense, President Park put his effort first into economic development. His thought was to build up the economy first and then lay the basis for security on that foundation.

In particular, the Blue House attack by North Korean commandos on January 21, 1968,[10] the appearance and disappearance of commandos in Uljin and Samcheok, and the American spy ship USS Pueblo incident[11] among other North Korean provocations further solidified President Park's will to pursue independent national defense, and this led to the creation of the Homeland Reserve Forces.

At that time, the reality of the situation was such that we could not manufacture even a single rifle and were completely dependent on the US for national defense. Our situation was so dire that President Park ordered a fundraiser for a helicopter at a joint conference between the administration and the ruling party.

The story is widely known among national security

insiders that President Park, provoked by the January 21st Blue House attack and further convicted to develop weapons independently, called then Minister of Economic Development Kim Hak-ryul, created plans to build four large main factories, and secretly ordered weapons manufacturing.

In this way, four major factories were quickly chosen and the development of artillery, grenades, and other weapons commenced. Soon after, the nationally manufactured weapons demonstration shooting competition was implemented under the direction of President Park. The demonstration, however, ended in a bitter comedy when an artillery shell meant to hit the mountain on the opposite side of the gallery landed right in front of the observation deck on which the President was seated. Yet, President Park did not waver in his commitment to independent weapons production.

Going without Dinner to Dispute with Agnew over US Troop Withdrawal

A sense of urgency about national security hit

President Park when President Nixon announced his "Guam Doctrine" in 1969. When Vice President Spiro Agnew visited Korea on August 24th of the following year, he made the deeply shocking announcement that of the two armies stationed in Korea, the 7th Army would withdraw and he could not guarantee that the remaining 2nd Army would not withdraw after June 1972.

At the time, during his talks with Vice President Agnew at the Blue House, President Park pressed for modernization of Korean Armed Forces first and withdrawal of US Troops later. That he held a fierce debate with Vice President Agnew, even skipping dinner, is a famous story.

Following that meeting, President Park's firm resolution was that national security had to dispense with American support, and ultimately, "We must defend our nation and our land with our own hands."

In 1971, the US 7th Army withdrew completely from the peninsula. The US military also retreated to the second line from the 155 mile-long ceasefire line, and the Korean troops took their place on the frontline.

After the withdrawal of the 7th Army, the US promised 150 million dollars in support without compensation, but it dragged on for 7 years and ended with only 90 million dollars.

President Park anticipated from the American attitude that in the end they would also withdraw the remaining troops from Korea, and he spurred on the advancement of the defense industry.

Spurring on the Defense Industry after the Fall of Saigon

The banner of defense industry advancement and independent national defense rolled out in earnest on April 30, 1975, after the fall of Saigon, which had been deemed impregnable to enemy invasion.

Many American scholars predicted that it was possible to preserve the South Vietnamese government through negotiations with North Vietnam, but their promise fell apart. Encouraged by the situation, North Korea's Kim Il-sung went back and forth to Beijing, bent on invading the South. At that time, President Park first eliminated the main causes of political instability by invoking Emergency Measure No. 9 and creating the civilian reserve defense, and he announced without hesitation that "We are confident that we will annihilate North Korea if they invade the South."

When the economy reached a level of stability, President Park focused on advancing the defense industry. Emphasizing that weapons production also required economic efficiency, he avoided production in arms factories like Taiwan and North Korea, and did not hesitate to delegate it to regular business corporations.

He first lured back to Korea topnotch talents who had studied abroad. At the time, military experts in the US and Japan who observed the make-up of the recruited talent pool even said in agreement, "Korea has sufficient capacity to develop nuclear or advanced precision weapons."

Korea did not even have design plans for weapons production. The US was stingy with providing plans. Take for example the Vulcan cannon production. We completely disassembled the 20 cannons supplied to us by the Americans, and after other countless hardships, we took this as the basis for making a much more capable weapon. Only after it became possible for us to produce them on our own, the US would give us the design plans.

Inspiring Confidence in the People on Countering North Korea

While President Park nurtured the defense industry, he did not lag behind in nurturing the will for reunification in the people, saying, "If a tragedy like 6.25[12] happens again, it is certain that reunification of our country will be delayed by decades or even centuries. Hence, we must be fully prepared with a mindset to demolish them at first battle in the likelihood of such an event."

This kind of dedication of President Park bore fruit. At the beginning-of-the-year press conference, President Park confidently announced, "We have exceeded North Korea in every area."

Up to that time, South Korea could not avoid falling behind on national defense expenditure, but it had grown at the same scale as the North by 1975.

US support, however, had become so unreliable with each passing day that the situation amounted to an emergency. Candidate Carter who was the challenger for the American Presidency presented as his campaign promise the complete withdrawal of all US troops from Korea and dismantling of the nuclear base. After he won the election, he sent Under Secretary of State Philip Habib and Chairman George Brown of the Joint Chiefs of Staff to give notice of complete withdrawal of US troops stationed in Korea, and hastened the actual withdrawal process.

Ahead of this, President Carter called Minister of Foreign Affairs Park Dong-jin to Washington immediately after his inauguration and notified him that there was no change in his promise to withdraw.

President Park, however, received the notice calmly with the attitude that what was to come has come, and he pledged, “The theme of this policy is consistent with the President Nixon’s Guam Doctrine. From now on, let us resolve even more to prepare perfectly all that is required for independent national defense.”

Adhering to the principle, “Prepare for everything, and there is no worry,” President Park instilled in the people the confidence that they will certainly beat North Korea in a one-on-one contest if the US kept just the Korea-US mutual defense treaty.

Taking in the reality of the situation, President Park accelerated the collaboration for development of advanced precision weapons and the start of the Korea-US Combined Forces Command to deter tensions on the Korean Peninsula. In doing so, he actually succeeded in installing a mechanism for preventing US withdrawal.

On August 18, 1976, when North Korean soldiers killed with axes two American officers at the Joint Security Area in Panmunjom, UN Commander-in-Chief General Richard Stilwell and other high ranking American military experts marveled at President Park’s response.

At the time, the Americans showed signs that they wanted to regard this incident simply as a minor skirmish that can frequently happen at a ceasefire line.

President Park, however, insisted to General Stilwell,

"We must teach them a lesson," and in the end succeeded in putting the North Koreans in their place.

UN soldiers followed President Park's suggestion and removed the poplar tree that led to the trouble at Panmunjom, and the situation then swiftly went to the brink of war.

While all the citizens slept peacefully without any inkling of what was happening, the entire armed forces, not to mention the Blue House, went into high alert and prepared for any possible situation.

In the end, the matter was resolved for the time being with North Korea's Kim Il-sung communicating his 'regrets' to the UN Commander, and President Park's decisive action stopped North Korea's scheming to invade the South.

Everyone knows the famous story of how the UN Commander General Stilwell offered a commemoration plaque cut from the problematic poplar tree to President Park to thank him for his decisiveness.

On October 1st of that year, when his secretaries presented speeches for the Armed Forces Day, he took out his pen, as if to say he was not satisfied with any of them, and wrote the entire speech from the greeting "Beloved citizens" to the end. That was the famous speech where he said, "A crazy dog must be subdued with a club," and expressed a steely resolve and readiness to battle against North Korea.

President Park's will to achieve independent national defense and unrelenting courage and decisiveness are well known to high ranking American generals and military scholars.

When President Carter wanted to force the withdrawal, most generals stationed in Korea supported President Park's position instead of President Carter's, and General Singlove went so far as to criticize Carter openly and publicly. It is also well known that at the time, some of the high-ranking American generals could not contain their admiration and expressed the sentiment, "Only if our country could have a president like that…."

Someone like General Holling Seward was so impressed with President Park's notion of annihilation at first battle and "repelling the enemy at the present frontline," that he continued to hold him in admiration as a military expert even after he was transferred.

When UN Command's strategic plan was criticized for not including the Five Islands in the Yellow Sea, President Park's firm resolve led to two visits by General Stilwell to the Yellow Sea, recommendations for American national defense, and the decision to include the Five Islands in the strategic plan at the Korea-US security meeting that year.

UN Commander General John W. Vessey, who received a medal from President Park during President Carter's visit, supported President Park's position to such an extent that he privately confided, "I can't take this medal if there is no fundamental change to America's withdrawal policy."

The defense industry that began without a single design plan grew to the point that it could manufacture 155 millimeter artillery, vulcans, tanks, and missiles. The production was so precise that there was not a single error in 1,000 produced units, and it won the envy of other developing nations.

The Armed Forces Day event held at the Yeouido Plaza on October 1, 1978 was a celebration displaying to the world domestic equipment and domestic weapons. World military leaders invited to the event gaped and marveled at the superb quality of the weapons. Afterward, so many countries requested weapons technology and sales from us, so that it made the headlines of the foreign press who reported, "South Korea is exporting weapons." Our defense industry now has entered the stage of mass production of helicopters, M48A5 tanks, Sidewinder missiles, with only the exception of fighter jets.

After his transfer, former UN Commander General Stilwell portrayed President Park in his papers this way:

"What I felt every time I met him was the sense that no other politician would go to such lengths for his country. The urgent goals for Korea are, needlessly to say, prevention of war and creating a peaceful life. President Park has almost accomplished these goals, and he is devoting himself to completely fulfilling them. I am not trying unilaterally to praise him. As a former commander of an allied power who oversaw a part of Korea's defense, I am simply evaluating the Korean leader as he is."

When General Stilwell and his wife offered incense after President Park's memorial was set in the reception room of the Blue House, it was perhaps out of admiration and the hope that President Park's determination to achieve independent national defense would continue forever.

<*The Chosun Ilbo,* October 30, 1979>

5 The Resolve for Reunification

The Ultimate Goal and Faith of Governing

Leading Peace Negotiations through '8.15 Declaration'

For President Park Chung-hee, peaceful reunification of the Korean Peninsula was the ultimate goal of governing and an article of faith. The work of modernization that he forcefully promoted after the May 16 Revolution, spurring on the growth of national power, the lofty motto of independent national defense, establishment of the Yushin system were all related to the path to reunification.

In the beginning-of-the-year news conference on January 9, 1970, President Park declared, "The 1970s is a period when we must address more actively the problem of reunification, and the time to rapidly expand national strength in order to create the foundations and necessary conditions to prepare for it." He reminded us, "I recall that I once said the work of national modernization for me is an intermediary goal for national reunification."

This kind of outlook on the reunification issue did not change over many utterances and speeches both domestically and overseas, and at one time, President Park's conviction gave us a moving sense of walking through the streets of Pyeongyang after 25 years.

On August 30, 1972, what led to our witnessing the astonishing sight of Red Cross representatives of South and North Koreas(*Nambukjeok*)[13] meeting in Pyeongyang for the first time for negotiations over the separate families issue cannot be explained solely on the basis of changes in international relations, such as the thawing of US-China relations.

It must be seen as emerging from President Park's active initiatives after announcing the August 15th Peaceful Reunification Concept in 1970, based on the strengthening of systemic mechanisms such as the opening of the National Territory Unification

Department(March 1, 1969), until the first South-North face to face meeting. In this announcement, President Park declared, "I am prepared to present an epoch-making and realistic plan to dismantle in stages the artificial wall dividing South and North Koreas." He then asked, "Are you prepared to engage in a well-intentioned competition that demonstrates which system between democracy and communist dictatorship can give a better life to the people, and which society has the conditions to provide a better life?"

This 'well-intentioned competition' signifies a transitional peaceful co-existence, and the emphasis on 'peace' follows from the conviction that the people's extermination must be avoided at all costs.

As a war on the Korean Peninsula will certainly escalate into a nuclear war, President Park's earnest thought was that first a mechanism to avoid such a scenario must be prepared. Even before making the August 15th announcement, President Park always stressed, "No matter how desirable national reunification is, it cannot be achieved through war, and even if it takes time, we have to resolve the issue in stages." At the time, with North Korea pouring all its energy into expanding military strength through measures such as the Great Four-Point Military Policy, the continuing trend of defeat in the Vietnam War, and the declaration of the Nixon Doctrine, President Park was keenly aware that it was a time of crisis when Kim Il-Sung was looking for an opportune moment to invade militarily the South. He had to make a forceful decision to achieve the goal of peaceful reunification.

Secret Emissary Dispatched to Enemy Territory, Gave Birth to <July 4th Joint Statement>[14]

This decision is clearly demonstrated in secretly dispatching the then KCIA Director Lee Hu-rak to Pyeongyang after May 2, 1972. In order to alleviate tension and prevent war, a climate of mutual trust must first be created. The President took the initiative in creating trust by taking the risky decision to send Director Lee into enemy territory, and thereby found an opening in the blocked South-North relations.

One can hardly imagine President Park's struggles

before making the decision to send Mr. Lee to Pyeongyang. At the 1973 beginning-of-the-year press conference, President Park stated, "Sending Director Lee to Pyeongyang last year was a major risk. As I sent Director Lee to Pyeongyang, I reflected on the Three Kingdoms Era in our history...."

The President had not been able to sleep as he chewed over, a thousand years later, the ancient event in which Silla's Kim Chun-Chu visited by himself Pyeongyang of Goguryeo and became imprisoned.

However, Press Secretary Sun Woo-yun and Blue House spokesperson Im Bang-hyun said, "We had no idea that Director Lee went to Pyeongyang." They expressed their surprise when they found out about the situation only after President Park suddenly said, "I heard Director Lee took cyanide with him when he went to Pyeongyang," the day before the July 4 South-North Joint Statement was announced. After President Park finally decided to send Director Lee to Pyeongyang, he composed the 'Presidential Instructions for Special Territory Trip' on April 26 and dispatched it. In this instruction, President Park ordered the following points as the ‘Republic of Korea’s Basic Position’ to be presented to Kim Il-Sung:

- Reunification of the country must be ultimately a peaceful reunification through political talks
- Reunification must be accomplished by looking at the real state of mutual differences in structural organization in all areas after 25 years, and by resolving numerous issues
- Work to quickly resolve issues of humanity by accelerating the South-North talks in progress.
- Proceed from resolving nonpolitical issues such as the economy and culture to political issues
- In order to improve the state of South-North relations, reject unrealistic, unilateral, propagandistic proposals for reunification, and at the same time stop mutual attacks and slander between South and North domestically and internationally, and refrain from any attempt to harass one another by direct and indirect military actions

Staying in Pyeongyang from May 2, over 3 days and 4 nights, Director Lee held two rounds of talks with Kim Il-sung and Kim Young-joo, and gave birth to the July 4th Joint Statement, the only joint document to be issued between South and North after independence.

Current Democratic Republican Party Assemblymen Mr. Lee Hu-rak said about the talks, "When I reproached Kim Il-sung about the January 21 Blue House attack, Kim asked me to convey to President Park that it was deeply regretful incident and he will never make war in the future."

Lee stresses that if South-North talks did not begin at that time, war would have already broken out. The state in South and North in 1970 and 71 was such that North Korea was racing to prepare for war while we were making emergency preparations to deal with the threat. It was a situation in which we did not know when war would break out, whether by accident or not, said Lee. Although he did not know whether the secret dispatch would lead to losing his office in the worst case, was it not the case that President Park gave the instructions anyway solely out of love of country, said

Lee. Following Lee's Pyeongyang trip, Kim Il-sung sent down Park Sung-chul to Seoul.

When Park Sung-chul visited President Park at the Blue House on May 31, the President repeatedly said to Park, "The key to the success or failure of South-North talks lies in eliminating mutual mistrust, and we have to face squarely the real state of the South-North division and proceed in stages by resolving first easier issues that have feasible solutions," and his associates report that Park also expressed agreement. The crisis of war was ultimately resolved through President Park's bold decision, and the South-North talks flowered through the middle of 1973. It was because he decided to send Director Lee to Pyeongyang that the preparatory South-North talks could conclude and continue with the main talks, and the South-North Coordinating Committee[15] was born.

It is true that when the historical July 4th statement, which followed the South-North independent peaceful reunification principle, was announced, many citizens had the misunderstanding that South-North reunification would happen in a day or two. President

Park himself, however, never fell into rosy illusions and deeply worried about future progress from the beginning, reports his associates.

On the afternoon of July 4, a few hours after the July 4th statement was made public, President Park called together his secretarial assistants and pointing out that easy success in talks with communists has almost never happened in history, he ordered, "As they will break away from the talks and try to cast the blame on us in the worst case scenario, research countermeasures in preparation for that," report his assistants. Unfortunately, President Park's prediction unerringly came true.

Before and after the fourth main South-North summit in November 1972, the North restarted slandering the South and dispatching spies, and travel to Pyeongyang from our side ended after the final fifth summit in March 1973. Despite our side's continuous efforts, the North Korean side unilaterally announced in Kim Young-joo's name the termination of the South-North Coordinating Committee.

In this announcement, Kim Young-joo mentioned the

Kim Dae-jung incident, and criticized President Park's June 23rd Peaceful Reunification Diplomacy Policy announcement as the "public declaration of the second Chosun battle front," presenting these as the reasons for termination.

The essential points of President Park's June 23rd announcement were:

- On the basis of the July 4th Joint Statement, we will continue the South-North talks with sincerity and patience
- We will not oppose North Korea jointly participating with us in international organizations if this contributes to alleviation of tensions and international cooperation
- We will not oppose simultaneous membership in the UN
- Under the principle of mutual benefit, both nations open their doors

North Korea casting blame on the June 23rd announcement can be nothing but an absurd ploy.

Regarding North Korea's attitude, even as President Park analyzed the situation saying, "They agreed to the South-North talks because they wanted to use it to rouse public opinion in America and first make the US troops in Korea withdraw, but they broke it off when this failed," he expressed his determination to his associates that "we must continue talking."

President Park said, "When seen in light of the ultimate goal of reunification, the South-North Coordinating Committee and the opening of the South-North summit already hold huge significance," and repeatedly promised, "When the time comes, we will change the entire set of representatives from both sides, and press to find a way to restart the talks," said Assemblymen Sun Woo-yun, conveying President Park's thoughts at the time.

To President Park, as he made clear in the message he sent to his Northern compatriot in early January before the August 15th announcement in 1970, reunion of the people was a historical necessity that he believed would definitely happen, and in the beginning-of-the-year press conference in 1974, he proposed concluding a nonaggression agreement between South and North Koreas.

'Peace First – Reunification Second' as Major Theme, Promoted South-North Talks with Sense of Calling

Despite lack of response from the North Korean side, on August 15th of that year, President Park presented again the three major principles of peaceful reunification.

In order to fulfill the people's wish for peaceful reunification, President Park stated that the establishment of peace on the Korean Peninsula and South-North nonaggression agreement must be concluded. At the same time, he stated that if the opening of the doors between South and North and the restoration of trust are successfully achieved, fair election management and comprehensive free elections based on native population ratio must be implemented. President Park's major theme "Peace first, reunification second" is indeed the most reasonable and realistic reunification plan, considering the reality of the situation on the Korean Peninsula after 25 years of division.

President Park's strong insistence on South-North open door policy and exchange was based on the very obvious judgment that there was no other means of ultimately integrating a people who had grown so disparate. Finally, President Park made the epoch-making proposal on January 19 of this year, "Let's have the South and the North meet with each other and talk without any assumptions or conditions, whatever the time, place, and level." However, with North Korea, which adheres to the 'reunification war strategy', insisting on holding a mass meeting of the entire peoples and denying the existence of the Coordinating Committee, this proposal led to only a few irregular face-to-face meetings.

On the failure of his January 19 proposal to garner any results, President Park is said to have told his associates, "We must never be disappointed." President Park was confident that even though the North Korean side could not receive the proposal for talks as sincere because they could not suddenly change the motto 'South Chosun Liberation', which has continued for decades, to 'South-North Co-existence', once our side's gross economic output and defense industry became superior and exceeded theirs, they would have to open their doors, even if just to survive.

Accordingly, it is said that President Park always commented that by the 1980s when our national strength expands and breaks 50 billion US dollars in exports, the energy for South-North reunification will ripen. His associates say that President Park took it as his calling the duty to prevent war by any means until that time. President Park's 'reunification resolve' could be seen in building the Tongiljeon[16] in Gyeongju in 1977.

What, however, we must pay attention to is not only the 'resolve' but the fact that he prepared the foundation of national strength to make possible to some degree the South-North talks. We must remember it is a fact that after independence until the end of the 1960s, proposals for talks or interchange took place at North Korea's initiative, and in March 1964 the North Korean side, feeling a sense of shame at President Park's offer of food assistance, even promised, albeit absurdly, to provide annually 2 billion tons of rice.

<*The Chosu*n *Ilbo*, October 30, 1979>

Note

[Preface]

1. **President Park Chung-hee (1917-1979):** The 5th–9th President of Republic of Korea. A major general in the Army in 1961, he led the May 16 military coup d'état and afterward took power. By passing the Yushin (restoration) Constitution in October 1972 and other means, he held power over the long-term for 18 years. On October 26, 1979, he passed away after CIA director Kim Jae-Gyu shot him. His record achievements in economic advancement and national modernization through the Five-Year Economic Development Plan, New Community Movement (*Saemaul Undong*), and other measures during his presidency are seen as his most outstanding accomplishments.
2. **Kim Jae-gyu, Director of Korea Central Intelligence Agency (KCIA):** On October 26, 1979, during his tenure as the KCIA director, he shot to death President Park Chung-hee, Security Service director Cha Ji-Chul, and others, and initiated the 'October 26 incident'. He was arrested and executed.
3. **Cha Ji-chul, Director of the Security Service:** As a captain in 1961, he took part in the May 16 military coup d'état, became a member of the National Assembly, and then served as the Security Service director. During his tenure, he was shot by KCIA director Kim Jae-gyu and was killed.
4. **May 16 Coup d'état:** A military coup d'état led by Park Chung-hee on May 16, 1961, soldiers who had graduated as the 8th class of the Korea Military Academy dismantled The Second Republic by force and took over the government.
5. **Celebrity singer:** Shim Soo-bong. First generation woman singer and songwriter in Korea. She gained popularity after participating in the MBC College Song Festival in 1978 with 'That Person Back Then'. The following year, she was invited to the Gungjeong-dong party where she became embroiled in the October 26 incident while singing and suffered hardship. Since then, she has recorded hits such as 'I Know Nothing but Love' and 'Men are Ships, Women are Ports', and continues to be active.
6. **Young model:** Shin Jae-soon. While working as a model during college, she was invited to the Gungjeong-dong party on October 26, became embroiled in the Park Chung-hee assassination incident, and underwent hardship.

7. **Presidential Secretary:** Kim Gye-won. As Chief Secretary to President Park Chung-hee, he became involved in the October 26, 1979 incident, received life imprisonment for murder with intent to commit insurrection and attempting to commit key insurrectionist activities, but was freed in 1982.
8. **Korean Armed Forces Capital Hospital:** Highest level medical institute among military hospitals treating military officers.

[Appendix 1: President Park's Last Words]

1. **National Security Agency:** former name of the National Intelligence Service, it is the national intelligence organization directly under the President's authority, responsible for affairs related to intelligence, security, and criminal investigations.
2. **Safe House:** Refers to residential houses used for the purposes of maintaining secrecy in administration or investigations of government or special intelligence organizations such as the Blue House or the National Intelligence Service.
3. **The Blue House:** The official residence of the President of Korea, situated in Jongno-gu, Seoul.
4. **August 15 Independence Day:** Officially designated national holiday celebrated every August 15, it commemorates independence from Japanese occupation on August 15, 1945.
5. **Young-soo:** Yuk Young-soo, President Park Chunghee's wife. When Park Chunghee was elected president in 1963, she developed a variety of social and education projects. On August 15, 1974, at the Independence Day Commemoration event, which opened at the National Central Theater, she was assassinated on the platform by Moon Sae-kwang of the General Association of Korean Residents in Japan (*Jochongryon*).
6. **Son:** Park Ji-man. Park Chung-hee and Yuk Young-soo's only son. At the time of Park's death, he was a cadet at the Korean Military Academy.
7. The Korean word translated as "common man" here is "pil-bu" (匹夫), which connotes a person of low social status and little achievement.
8. **Bu-Ma Democratic Protests:** Protests against Park Chung-hee's Yushin (restoration) dictatorship, centered around the Busan and Masan area, in

October 1979.

9. ***Baek-ui-minjok:*** Literally "white clothed people," a name for Korean people that originated long ago for their custom of wearing and holding in esteem white clothes.

10. **Kim Ilsung:** North Korean politician. From 1948 to his death in 1994, he established a system of cult of personality by monopolizing power as the Government Premier and Head of the Nation, and by starting the June 25 Korean War solidified the South-North division. He is the grandfather of Kim Jong-Un, Chairman of the North Korean Workers' Party and Chairman of the State Affairs Commission.

11. **[Translator's note]:** *Gat*, a traditional black hat made out of bamboo.

12. **Yushin:** President Park Chung-hee announced martial law and passed the Yushin Constitution in 1972 under the pretext of proactively addressing the division between North and South Koreas and the changes in international relations. As a result, he greatly expanded presidential powers and limited citizens' rights.

13. **Army Chief of Staff:** Jung Seung-hwa, Chief of Staff during the incident on October 26, 1979.

14. **[Translator's note]** Namsan is a mountain located within Seoul.

15. "Barley hump" (*borit gogae*) refers to the period between May and June when the food from the fall harvest has run out and the barley has not yet ripened, making the food situation very difficult on the farms.

16. **Daughters:** Park Chung-hee and Yuk Young-soo had two daughters, Park Geun-hye and Park Geun-ryeong. Park Geun-hye was the 18th President of Korea.

17. **Moraesil:** A local name for Park Chung-hee's birthplace. The actual name of his village is Sangmori in the town of Gumi, North Gyeongsang Province, but for a long time the local people called it Moraesil.

18. **[Translator's note]** *"Jangi"* is a strategy board game that has similarities with chess and commonly called 'Chinese chess'.

19. **[Translator's note]** *"Jegi"* is a tassled ball used in traditional folk games played by children, similar to a hacky sack.

[Appendix 2: President Park Chung-hee, His Dedication and Legacy]

1. ***Chosun Ilbo:*** A comprehensive daily newspaper first published on March 5, 1920. As of 2019, Chosun Ilbo is the largest newspaper and ranks first among Korean daily news publications in terms of the official number of printed copies and sales.
2. **New Community Movement (*Saemaul Undong*):** Rural reform movement that was carried out in early 1970 after President Park Chung-hee discussed a new community movement at the national provincial ministers' meeting and followed up with concrete implementation. Initially, Saemaul Undong was only a movement to increase agricultural profit, but as it garnered much success, it spread to urban centers, factories, and employers and developed into a consciousness reform movement that promoted industriousness, self-reliance, and collaboration in daily life. It was a government-led national modernization movement that instilled a strong determination in the people to achieve economic independence and make it as an advanced nation without fail.
3. **[Translator's note]** Gangwon-do, northeast province of South Korea.
4. ***Tongil* rice:** A newly created rice variety that was cultivated by crossbreeding Indica and Japonica rice by working and researching night and day, an effort led by the then biology researcher Professor Hur Moon-hwae under President Park's order in 1970 to solve the food crisis and the problem of food self-sufficiency. The rice was a high yield variety that had around 30% higher production than other types, and by gradually increasing the cultivation area for Tongil rice, the country recorded 113% in rice self-sufficiency in 1977.
5. **Gyeongbu Highway:** A highway connecting Seoul to Busan, it is called the 'major artery of Republic of Korea's road traffic' as it has the most amount of traffic and is the longest single route in Korea. Construction began on February 1, 1968 and finished on July 7, 1970. On August 31, 1971, its name was designated as the Seoul-Busan Expressway.
6. **Park Chung-hee's state visit to West Germany:** At the time, West Germany was displaying remarkable economic growth and needed a larger labor pool. In 1963, Park Chung-hee promoted sending Korean workers such as miners and nurses, and their hard-earned foreign currency was used as seed money for Korean economic revival. When Park Chung-hee visited West Germany in 1964, he met and consoled the miners and nurses who had been sent.

7. **Eo Jae-yeon (1823-1871)**: General in Late Joseon period. During the French and American invasions, he led the fight against the forces attacking the beaches of Gwangha Island and defended the country. He is especially remembered for intensely fighting against 1,230 American troops and their five battleships with only 600 soldiers and dying heroically.
8. **King Sejong (1397-1450):** Fourth King of Joseon Dynasty, the period of his rule was the golden age of Korean history when the foundations for politics, economics, society, and culture were comprehensively established, and the best Confucian politics and brilliant cultural life flourished. Through the Jiphyeonjeon (Hall of Worthies) research institute, many people of talent were raised up; ceremonies and institutions that form the basis of Confucian rule were improved; the Korean alphabet was invented; agriculture, science, and technology advanced; medical knowledge, music, and law were systematized; and territory expanded. Through many such projects, his rule fortified the foundations of the country.
9. **Chungmugong Hyeonchungsa:** A shrine that preserves the portrait of the Joseon Dynasty Admiral Chungmogong Yi Sun-shin (1545-1598) and commemorates his accomplishments. Yi Sun-shin was the Naval Commander of the three southern islands who led the navy against the invading Japanese forces, winning every battle and achieving great merit for the country. He is a national symbol and is revered as one of the greatest figures in Korean history.
10. The incident refers to the attack on the Blue House by 31 members of the 124th regiment of the North Korean special forces on January 21, 1968. It is also called the "Kim Shin-Jo Incident" after the only commando to be captured alive, Kim Shin-Jo.
11. **The Pueblo Incident**: On January 23, 1968, the American spy ship USS Pueblo was captured by a North Korean naval patrol ship in international waters near Wonsan port in North Korea.
12. **The Korean War:** Referred to by its date, June 25, 1950, when North Korean troops crossed the South-North military borderline at the 38th parallel and illegally invaded the South. The war ultimately conflagrated into an international proxy war with UN troops and Chinese People's Army participating, and continued until it was concluded by an armistice agreement on July 27, 1953, three years and one month after it began. Due to this war, countless civilians and soldiers lost their lives, almost all the industrial infrastructure was destroyed, and the economy was razed to the

ground. The war became the decisive opportunity for solidifying the state of division on the Korean Peninsula.

13. ***Nambukjeok:*** Red Cross of South and North Koreas working to resolve the issue of 10,000,000 families separated by the South-North division. In 1971, South-North Red Cross representatives began meeting, and the first historical separated families meeting took place in 2001, followed by 21 meetings until 2018.

14. **July 4th South-North Joint Statement:** A historical joint statement on reunification issued by South and North Koreas for the first time after division on July 4, 1972.

15. **South-North Coordinating Committee:** A body for political discussions between the Northern and Southern authorities, it was established for achieving the goals of promoting the points of agreements in the 'July 4th South-North Joint Statement', improving and advancing South-North relations, and resolving the reunification issue.

16. **Tongiljeon (Unification Hall):** Built in 1977, it commemorates the unification of the Three Kingdoms, and the great accomplishments of King Taejong Muyeol, King Munmu, and General Kim Yu-Shin, and supplicates for South and North reunification.

30/50 Club
A Dialogue on S. Korea, U.S., China, and N. Korea

Date of publication 2019. 7. 10

 Published by Korean Literature Inc.,
281 Dokmak-ro, Mapo-gu, Seoul.

TEL 02-706-8541~3 | **FAX** 02-706-8544
E-mail hkmh73@hanmail.net
Blog http://blog.naver.com/hkmh1973
Publishing registration 1979. 8. 3. 300-1979-24

ISBN 978-89-87527-79-6 03810